SAINT MACARIUS THE SPIRITBEARER

Coptic Texts Relating to Saint Macarius the Great

ST VLADIMIR'S SEMINARY PRESS
Popular Patristics Series

Editor
JOHN BEHR

Saint Macarius the Spiritbearer

Coptic Texts Relating to Saint Macarius the Great

Translated, with Introduction, by

TIM VIVIAN

ST VLADIMIR'S SEMINARY PRESS
CRESTWOOD, NEW YORK
2004

Library of Congress Cataloging-in-Publication Data

Histoire des monastères de la Basse-Egypt. English.
   Saint Macarius, the spiritbearer : coptic texts relating to Saint Macarius the Great / translated, with introduction by Tim Vivian.
        p.   cm. — (St. Vladimir's Seminary Press's "popular patristics" series)
   Includes bibliographical references and index.
   ISBN 0–88141–257–0 (alk. paper)
   1. Macarius, the Egyptian, Saint, 4th cent.   2. Macarius, the Egyptian, Saint, 4th cent.—Quotations.   I. Vivian, Tim.   II. Title.   III. Series.

BR65.M336H5713 2004
270.2'092—dc22

                                                                              2004020366

"We cannot let modern questions about historicity divert us from understanding how memory worked in early monastic communities. Those communities, from all indications, did take great pains to remember accurately. But it was not accuracy for accuracy's sake. It was not the accuracy that might move a modern historian, or one that might have moved an ancient historian. It was accuracy for the sake of spirituality. . . . Its concern was not past facts, but past wisdom that might serve the present quest."

—William Harmless, S.J.

In Memoriam

Emile Amélineau

H. I. Bell

E. A. Wallis Budge

Derwas J. Chitty

René-Georges Coquin

W. E. Crum

Hugh G. Evelyn White

Jean-Claude Guy

shoulders

Contents

Foreword

Ten years ago Gabriel Bunge and Adalbert de Vogüé published a groundbreaking work, based on previously published articles by the two authors, *Quatre ermites égyptiens: d'après les fragments coptes de l'Histoire Lausiaque* (Spiritualité Orientale 60; Bégrolles-en-Mauges: Bellefontaine, 1994). In this volume they offer a French translation of four monastic *Lives*, preserved in Coptic (the Coptic Palladiana), that are clearly related to the Greek *Lausiac History* of Palladius but that also differ dramatically from the same *Lives* in the Greek *History*. The four are: Pambo, Evagrius, Macarius of Egypt (Macarius the Great), and Macarius of Alexandria. Vogüé provides translations based on much improved texts, while Bunge, in a thorough introduction, discusses the relationship between the Coptic *Lives* and the *Lausiac History* and argues for their importance as primary documents witnessing to the early years of Egyptian monasticism.

The paired volumes offered here—*Four Desert Fathers* and *Saint Macarius the Spiritbearer*—began as an effort to bring the fruits of Bunge and Vogüé's work to a wider audience, to offer English translations of the four Coptic *Lives* and provide an introduction to them that, in part, distills the work of Bunge and Vogüé and makes these works more accessible to a modern audience. *Four Desert Fathers* thus offers translations of these four Coptic *Lives*, preceded by an Introduction. The four were originally published separately in different form in the *Coptic Church Review*; I wish to thank the *Review* and its editor, Rodolph Yanney, M.D., for ceding the copyright to me and thus making them available for publication.

As my work progressed on *Four Desert Fathers*, I saw that three other Coptic texts relating to Saint Macarius the Great also deserved to be translated into English and should form a separate volume: as supplements to the Coptic Palladiana, but also as important documents in their own right. These three texts are *The Sayings of Saint Macarius*, *The Virtues of Saint Macarius* (for which I supply corrections to the text edited by Amélineau), and *The Life of Saint Macarius of Scetis*. Translations of these three texts thus appear as this volume, *Saint Macarius the Spiritbearer*, which has its own Introduction. The *Sayings* appeared in a different form in *Cistercian Studies Quarterly* and selections of the *Virtues* appeared in *Hallel*; I wish to thank the editors of those journals, Fr Charles Cummings, OCSO, and Fr Ciarán Ó Sabhaois, OCSO, respectively, for their permission to reprint.

During the long and enjoyable gestation of this work I have had help and encouragement from a number of people. I wish especially to thank William Harmless, SJ for reading early drafts of each chapter, for his numerous suggestions, and above all for his support and encouragement. I wish to thank Monica Blanchard for her editorial assistance. My thanks to Rowan A. Greer for translating the Syriac text for Appendix II to *Four Desert Fathers*. Apostolos Athanassakis, Augustine Casiday, William Harmless, SJ, Dar Brooks Hedstrom, Maged Mikhail, Birger Pearson, Mark Sheridan, OSB, and Terry Wilfong helped with specific questions and each of them has my thanks. I wish to thank Jeffrey Russell for reading early drafts of the manuscript and offering numerous suggestions for improvement, and especially Adalbert de Vogüé, OSB, for reading the completed manuscript. Père Vogüé also graciously agreed to write a preface. I wish to thank Fr John Behr, editor of the Popular Patristics series at Saint Vladimir's Seminary Press, for reading the manuscript and making helpful suggestions.

The quotation at the front of this volume is from William Harmless, SJ, "Remembering Poemen Remembering: The Desert Fathers and the Spirituality of Memory," *Church History* 69:3 (2000): 483–518.

Finally, I wish to thank my family for their love and support: Miriam, Meredith, John, and David. And Amma Joyce, who is always asking what I'm working on.

The Feast of Saint Mary Magdalene, 2003

Tim Vivian
Bakersfield, California

Abbreviations

ACW   Ancient Christian Writers (New York: Paulist Press)

Am   É. Amélineau, *Histoire des monastères de la Basse-Égypte* (Annales du Musée Guimet, 25; Paris: Leroux, 1894)

AP   *Apophthegmata Patrum* (*Sayings of the Fathers*). [Alphabetical AP may be found in PG 65.71–440]

Butler   *The Lausiac History of Palladius*, ed. and trans. Cuthbert Butler (2 vols.; Cambridge: Cambridge UP, 1898 and 1904)

BV   Gabriel Bunge and Adalbert de Vogüé, *Quatre ermites égyptiens: d'après les fragments coptes de l'Histoire Lausiaque* (Spiritualité Orientale 60; Bégrolles-en-Mauges: Bellefontaine, 1994)

Chaîne   M. Chaîne, "La double recension de l'*Histoire Lausique* dans la version copte," *Revue de l'orient chrétien*, 25 (1925–26): 232–75

Crum   Walter Ewing Crum, *A Coptic Dictionary* (Oxford: Clarendon, 1939)

EH   *Ecclesiastical History* (by Eusebius, Rufinus, Socrates or Sozomen)

Evelyn White   Hugh G. Evelyn White, ed. by Walter Hauser, *The Monasteries of the Wâdi 'n Natrûn*, 3 vols. (New York: Metropolitan Museum of Art, 1926–1933 [repr. Arno Press: New York, 1973]). Part I: *New Coptic Texts from the Monastery of Saint Macarius*, Part II: *The History of the Monasteries of Nitria and Scetis*, Part III: *The Architecture and Archaeology*

Gk   Greek

Lampe   G. W. H. Lampe, *A Patristic Greek Lexicon* (Oxford: Clarendon, 1961)

LH	Palladius, *Lausiac History*
LSJ	Henry George Liddell and Robert Scott, rev. Henry Stuart Jones, *A Greek English Lexicon* (Oxford: Clarendon, 1968)
LXX	The Septuagint; *Septuaginta*, ed. Alfred Rahlfs (Stuttgart: Deutsche Bibelstiftung Stuttgart, 1935)
Meyer	*Palladius: The Lausiac History*, trans. Robert T. Meyer (New York: Newman Press, 1964)
PG	Patrologia Graeca
Ramsey	*John Cassian: The Conferences*, trans. by Boniface Ramsey (Mahwah, NJ: Paulist Press, 1997)
Regnault	Lucien Regnault, *Les Sentences des Pères du désert: Troisieme recueil et tables* (Solesmes, 1976)
Russell	*The Lives of the Desert Fathers: The Historia Monachorum in Aegypto*, trans. by Norman Russell (Kalamazoo: Cistercian, 1981)
SC	Sources chrétiennes (Paris: Cerf)
Vogüé	Adalbert de Vogüé, *Quatre ermites égyptiens: d'après les fragments coptes de l'Histoire Lausiaque* (Spiritualite Orientalé 60; Bégrolles-en-Mauges: Bellefontaine, 1994)
Ward	Benedicta Ward, trans., *The Sayings of the Desert Fathers: The Alphabetical Collection* (rev. ed.; Kalamazoo: Cistercian, 1984)

SAINT MACARIUS THE SPIRITBEARER

Introduction

Saint Macarius the Great

Macarius the Great, also called Macarius of Egypt or Macarius the Egyptian (to distinguish him from Macarius of Alexandria)[1] is one of the most venerated saints of the Coptic Church (his name, which means "blessed" in Greek, is "Makarios," in Arabic "Maqar"). He was born around the year 300 in Jijbēr (present-day Shabshîr), a village in the southwest portion of the Nile delta and, therefore, was a child during the Great Persecution (306–311) and a teenager when Constantine promulgated the Edict of Toleration in 313.[2] As a young man he was a camel driver; as part of his job as a gatherer of natron, he may have visited the Wadi al-Natrun, his future monastic home.[3] Still a young man, he became a village ascetic or anchorite, like Saint Antony and others before him.[4]

[1] In ancient monastic literature "Egypt" often stands in juxtaposition against (Greek) "Alexandria."

[2] Much of this biographical section is drawn from Antoine Guillaumont, "Macarius the Egyptian, Saint," *The Coptic Encyclopedia* (New York: Doubleday, 1991), 5.1491, and Hugh G. Evelyn White, *The Monasteries of the Wadi 'N Natrûn*, vol. 2, *The History of the Monasteries of Nitria and Scetis* (repr. New York: Arno, 1973), 60–72. On Macarius in the *AP*, see Jean-Claude Guy's discussion in his introduction to *Les Apophtegmes des Pères: Collection Systématique. Chapitres I–IX* (SC 387; Paris: Cerf, 1993), especially 47–49.

[3] The *Life of Macarius of Scetis* 7–8 records earlier visits. This *Life*, attributed to Sarapion of Thmuis, is independent of the Palladian *Life of Macarius of Egypt* (found in *Four Desert Fathers*, the companion volume to this one). Years later, Macarius' thievery as a young camel driver was still a reproof, and means of humility, for him. See *AP* Macarius the Great 31; Benedicta Ward, trans., *The Sayings of the Desert Fathers* (rev. ed.; Kalamazoo: Cistercian, 1984), 134.

[4] See *Life of Antony* 3–4; on village ascetics, see E. A. Judge, "The Earliest Use of

About 330 Macarius went to the Wadi al-Natrun (Scetis), south-west of the Nile delta, about the same time that Amoun was found-ing a monastic settlement just to the north in Nitria. Settling eventually near the site of the present-day monastery named in his honor, Deir Anba Maqar, Macarius at first lived alone.[5] Soon, how-ever, he began to attract disciples and a small community formed around him. By 340 a growing monastic settlement was solidly in place in Scetis; a mere sixteen years later, Abba Sisoës would leave Scetis for remoter regions, complaining that it was now too crowded.[6] Little more, however, is known for sure of either Macar-ius or his community at this time. Macarius apparently was made a priest ten years after coming to the Wadi al-Natrun. He was deported during the Arian persecution in 374 to an island in the delta, returned some time later to Scetis, and died about 390.[7] As with other monastic saints, his body underwent numerous adventures and movings about, coming to rest finally at Deir Anba Maqar, where it is venerated today.[8]

Macarius' life, as was often the case, soon became the stuff of leg-end.[9] In Coptic tradition Macarius was later hailed as "the first shoot

Monachos for 'Monk' (P. Coll. Youtie 77) and the Origins of Monasticism," *Jahrbuch für Antike und Christentum*, 20 (1977): 72–89, and James E. Goehring, *Ascetics, Soci-ety, and the Desert: Studies in Early Egyptian Monasticism* (Studies in Antiquity and Christianity; Harrisburg: Trinity, 1999), 13–35 and 53–72.

[5] For Macarius' earlier residences in Scetis, one of which may well have been what came to be called *Pa Romeos*, modern Baramus, "the [Monastery] of the Romans," see Evelyn White, 2.65, 102.

[6] *AP* Sisoes 28 (Ward, 218).

[7] See Rufinus *EH* 2.4, Palladius *LH* 17, and *AP* Macarius the Great 2 and 4 (Ward, 125, 128).

[8] See Father Matta el-Meskeen, *Coptic Monasticism and the Monastery of St. Macarius: A Short History* (Cairo: the Monastery of St. Macarius, 1984), 27–31, 53–54. On the removal of his remains from Scetis to Jijbēr, see the *Life of Macarius of Scetis* 37.

[9] For a full and judicious account of the material about Macarius, see Evelyn White, cited above. Evelyn White, 465–68, argues that the *Life of Macarius of Scetis* consists, for the most part, of "some fragments of surviving tradition floating in a sea of pious imagination" (468). Nevertheless, the *Life* contains historical elements (as Evelyn White acknowledges) and is an important hagiographical document.

of this vine ... that is Shiēt [Scetis]."[10] Macarius came to preside, in a loose manner, over the monks of Scetis. These monks were semi-anchoritic; that is, they lived alone or in small groups in scattered cells, and came together as a larger community usually only on Saturday and Sunday, when they celebrated the eucharist together and participated in a communal meal. We should not impose later structures, either architectural or monastic, on these monks: the monastic enclosure, with its high defensive walls, would not be the rule until the ninth century, and the rules and regulations of medieval Benedictine monasticism, much less the ways of modern orders, were unknown to them. The best way to understand these early monks, in any case, is not historically, but spiritually, through their thought and practices; the *Sayings* of the desert fathers and mothers offer the best access to their world.[11]

At their best, the early monks simplified the spiritual life to work and prayer, and erected no boundaries between these two, seeing them as integral parts of life in God.[12] In the same way, they numbered their spiritual precepts as two or three and not in the thousands: "Do no evil to anyone, and do not judge anyone. Observe this precept and you will be saved," offered Macarius.[13] Macarius taught that prayer did not require "long discourses; it is enough to stretch out one's hands and say, 'Lord, as you will, and as you know, have mercy.' And if the conflict grows fiercer say, 'Lord, help!'"[14] The

---

[10]*The Life of Maximus and Domitius*, in E. Amélineau, ed., *Histoire des monastères de la Basse Égypte* (Annales de Musée Guimet 25; Paris: Leroux, 1894), 263.

[11]Although there is no doubt that the *Apophthegmata* were compiled and edited later, there is also no doubt that they have their origins in the fourth century at Nitria and Scetis; for good recent discussions, see Graham Gould, *The Desert Fathers on Monastic Community* (Oxford: Clarendon, 1993), 1–25, and Douglas Burton-Christie, *The Word in the Desert: Scripture and the Quest for Holiness in Early Christian Monasticism* (New York and Oxford: Oxford, 1993), esp. 76–103 on the origins of the *Apophthegmata*, and Part III on spirituality.

[12]For a good discussion, see Lucien Regnault, *La vie quotidienne des pères du désert en Égypte au IVe siècle* (Paris: Hachette, 1990), esp. 109–16

[13]*AP* Macarius the Great 28 (Ward, 133).

[14]*AP* Macarius the Great 19 (Ward, 131).

monk was to become "a dead man." When a brother asked Macarius how to be saved, he told the monk to go to the cemetery and insult the dead; when the brother reported that he had done as he was told, Macarius then told him to go praise the dead. When the monk returned again, Macarius asked him, "Did they answer you?" When the monk said no, Macarius drove home his point: "You know how you insulted them and they did not reply, and how you praised them and they did not speak; so you too if you wish to be saved must do the same and become a dead man. Like the dead, take no account of either the scorn of men or their praises, and you can be saved."[15]

Such advice as Macarius gave to that monk may seem quaint to us today, unrealistic, but it is unrealistic in precisely the way that the Sermon on the Mount is "unrealistic": that is, it challenges us so profoundly that our usual defense is to dismiss it. In the same way, Macarius' actions are impossible, just as Jesus' are impossible. But Macarius, like Jesus, was known for his wonderworking: "The Egyptian had acquired such a reputation that he always had a disciple with him to receive 'clients' 'on account of the number of those who came to be healed by him.' "[16] One day Macarius discovered a man plundering his goods, "so he came up to the thief as if he was a stranger and he helped him to load the animal. He saw him off in great peace of soul."[17] It is worth noting that Macarius assists his thieves while quoting Scripture: "We have brought nothing into this world, and we cannot take anything out of the world" (1 Tim 6:7). Such detachment, ancient monasticism shows again and again, can lead to real peace.

[15] *AP* Macarius the Great 23 (Ward, 132).
[16] Regnault, 233.
[17] *AP* Macarius the Great 18 (Ward, 131); see also 40 (Ward, 137–38).

The Sayings of Saint Macarius of Egypt

Befitting his renown in antiquity, Macarius the Great has 41 sayings attributed to him in the Greek alphabetical collection of the *Apoph-thegmata Patrum* or *Sayings of the Desert Fathers [and Mothers]*, the second largest number (after Poemen). The Coptic collection is smaller, with 34 sayings (a synoptic table is provided in chap. 1 below). The two collections have 23 sayings in common: the Coptic lacks 18 sayings found in Greek while it has 11 sayings that the Greek lacks. These 11 additional sayings give the Coptic collection imme-diate value since they provide supplementary information about the saint. The most striking aspect of the two collections is the disparity between the way they order the sayings. Imagine the Greek collec-tion as a deck of 41 cards, with each saying a card; remove 18 cards and add 11 different ones; now shuffle them. The resulting order would not be dissimilar from the sequence of the Coptic collection vis-à-vis the Greek. The differences between the two collections with regard to number, order, and textual variants raise interesting ques-tions about the editing of the *Apophthegmata*, which probably took place in Palestine (not in Egypt) in the sixth century.

It would be a mistake to make the *a priori* assumption that the Greek text is always preferable to the Coptic. While the Coptic say-ings are undoubtedly translations from Greek, it is not automatically certain that they are translations based on the Greek text we have now; some may in fact preserve earlier or better readings. Saying 14 offers an example where the Coptic text is secondary: Abba Macar-ius told the brothers, "Flee, brothers," and an old man said to him, "Where shall we flee beyond this desert?" Macarius placed his finger on his mouth (that is, to his lips) and said, "This is flight." The Cop-tic text then adds a gloss, absent from the Greek, which explains that Macarius was indicating to the monks to safeguard silence. Saying 9, however, may preserve a better reading in Coptic. A pagan priest tells Macarius, "You have a great god on your side," whereas in Greek the priest says, "God is on your side." A pagan was probably more likely to say the former than the latter, and it easy to see how "a great god" could have been changed to "God" during the transmission of the saying. Sayings 20 and 21 are intriguing in that they are the only two told in the first person (third person in Greek), a possible indication of an early form of the sayings.[18]

Whatever the textual considerations, the Macarius of both the Greek and Coptic sayings is manifestly the same person.[19] Here I will look at only a few differences between the Greek and Coptic collections. One striking characteristic of the Coptic *Sayings* is that, unlike the Greek collection (4, 26) and the *Virtues of Saint Macarius*,[20] they do not show any connection between Macarius and Antony the Great, which is surprising. Nor do they include the famous story of Macarius assisting thieves in plundering his goods (Greek 18, and 40, its doublet).[21] It is difficult, if not impossible, to imagine that a scribe or editor would drop these sayings; they must have been absent from the Greek manuscript from which the Coptic translation was made.

The eleven additional Coptic sayings are not as a whole different from their Greek counterparts: they include a healing (7), an encounter with a demon (32), and sundry sayings (e.g., 18, 19, 28). Saying 27, however, has a striking addition to the corresponding Greek text, one that is worth noting. In this saying a monk sins and

[18]Antoine Guillaumont, "L'Enseignement spirituel des moines d'Égypte" repr. in his *Études sur la spiritualité de l'orient chrétien* (Begrolles-en-Mauges: Bellefontaine, 1996), 81–92, has shown, 85–86, how the *Apophthegmata* moved from first person and attributed accounts to third person, unattributed accounts.

[19]On Macarius in the *Apophthegmata*, see Jean-Claude Guy's discussion in his introduction to *Les Apophtegmes des Pères*, especially 47–49. Two good studies on Macarius of Egypt and Macarius of Alexandria are Antoine Guillaumont, "Le problème des deux Macaires dans les *Apophthegmata Patrum*," *Irénikon*, 48 (1975): 41–59, and Gabriel Bunge, "Évagre le Pontique et les deux Macaires," *Irénikon*, 56 (1983): 215–27, 323–60.

[20]"Vertus de Saint Macaire," in Amélineau ed., *Histoire des monastères de la Basse-Égypte*. Amélineau provides a French translation of the *Virtues*; see chap. 2 below for an English translation.

[21]This lends support to Antoine Guillaumont's intuition that that story is about Macarius the Alexandrian as opposed to Macarius the Egyptian; see his comments in "Le problème des deux Macaire," 55.

receives a penance from Macarius of Alexandria; still troubled, however, partly because he cannot carry out the assigned penance, the monk goes to "the other Abba Macarius, the Egyptian," who "calmed the brother's spirit and encouraged him in numerous ways, saying, 'Go, my child. That which you are able to do, do; gird yourself not to ever commit that sin again.'" At first this portion, which the Greek lacks, might seem to be a hagiographic improvement highlighting Macarius' compassionate pastoral care. But the saying (in both languages) contains implicit criticism of the Alexandrian's severity. More importantly, the compassion that Macarius evinces is amply corroborated in both the *Sayings* and the *Virtues* and seems to have been one of the chief things remembered about Macarius, along with his related teaching about God's mercy.[22] One saying attributed to him in the *Virtues* is particularly memorable:

> A brother asked Abba Macarius, "My father, I have fallen into a transgression."
>
> Abba Macarius said to him, "It is written, my son, 'I do not desire the death of a sinner as much as his repentance and his life' [see 1 Tim 2:4 and 2 Pet 3:9]. Repent, therefore, my son; you will see him who is gentle, our Lord Jesus Christ, his face full of joy towards you, like a nursing mother whose face is full of joy for her child when he raises his hands and his face up to her. Even if he is full of all kinds of uncleanness, she does not turn away from that bad smell and excrement but takes pity on him and lifts him up and presses him to her breast, her face full of joy, and everything about him is sweet to her. If, then, this created person has pity for her child, how much greater is the love of the creator, our Lord Jesus Christ, for us![23]

---

[22]See *Virtues* 9, 23, 25, 38, 43, and 70; Amélineau, "Vertus," 128–30, 142–43, 143–44, 156–57, 161–63, 187–88.

[23]*Virtues* 23; Amélineau, "Vertus," 142–43.

The deep love that Macarius demonstrates here, for both God and humanity, gives these sayings continuing power.

The Virtues of Saint Macarius of Egypt

The *Virtues of Saint Macarius* (chap. 2 below), written in Bohairic Coptic, exists in a single tenth-century manuscript; it may have survived because its chapters were used as a monastic lectionary.[24] No Greek or (more likely) Sahidic Coptic exemplar survives. Without the Greek, or a Latin translation, the work was confined to Egypt and is unknown in the West outside of a small circle of scholars.[25] The date (or, more accurately, dates) of the work is unknown. There appear to be two dateable events in the *Virtues*. In *Virtues* 32, Saint Shenoute the Great (d. 450) visits "the holy place of our father" (presumably the Monastery of Saint Macarius, modern Deir Anba Maqar) after the council of Ephesus in 431, some forty years after Macarius' death. Although the story is hagiographical, with the airborn Shenoute first seeing the monastery from on high, other sources do confirm that Shenoute attended Ephesus with Archbishop Cyril of Alexandria.[26] *Virtues* 16 has Macarius prophesying about the decline of monasticism after the first two destructions of Scetis in 407–8 and 434. These two stories would seem to place the compiling of the *Virtues* in the middle of the fifth century, about fifty years after Macarius' death.

Since there is no anti-Chalcedonian polemic in the *Virtues*, it seems likely that they were edited, in the main, before the Council of

[24]Cod. Vat LXIV, fol. 57–112. The text was edited by E. Amélineau, "Vertus de Saint Macaire" (see n. 20 above). At the top of the MS. it reads: "The second Sunday of Lent to the forty-sixth chapter of the book: read." There are other lectionary indications in the MS.; see the notes to the translation below.

[25]Evelyn White, in his monumental study, *The Monasteries of the Wadi 'N Natrûn*, does not discuss the *Virtues* in any detail.

[26]See *The Life of Shenoute by Besa*, trans. David N. Bell (Kalamazoo: Cistercian, 1983), 16–18, and the references cited. On Ephesus, see *Life of Shenoute* 128–30 (Bell, 78–79).

Chalcedon (451). *Virtues* 57 complicates matters by apparently leaping ahead two hundred years; it seems to contain references to Islam or the Arabs which, if taken as prophecy *ex eventu*, would place the composition of at least this one pericope after the Arab invasion of Egypt in 641. Some of the *Virtues* seem to point to an early form of the Jesus Prayer (see #13, 34, 35, 41, 42, and 44) and scholars have suggested that this stratum of the material belongs to the 6th, 7th, or 8th centuries.[27] The *Virtues* is undoubtedly a composite work, edited from perhaps the 5th through the 7th or 8th centuries. The roots of the *Virtues* as a whole, however, go much deeper, into the oral and written collections of monastic sayings of the fourth and fifth century known as the *Apophthegmata Patrum*. Some of the *Virtues*, how many it is impossible to say, indubitably go back to the earliest traditions of the desert fathers; some undoubtedly take us back to Saint Macarius himself and to the community that grew up around him.

The most immediately striking aspect of this collection of stories and sayings by and about Macarius is how little contact it has with the rest of the Macarian corpus: the *Sayings of Saint Macarius* (in Greek and Coptic) and the *Life of Macarius of Scetis* (Coptic only).[28] Of the eighty-two sayings as numbered here, only eight have parallels with the Greek *Sayings* and six with the Coptic; of these, only one (#6) has parallels with both.[29] (See the Synoptic Table at the beginning of Chapter One.) By way of contrast, almost two-thirds of the Coptic *Sayings of Saint Macarius* have parallels with the Greek *Sayings*.

[27]Antoine Guillaumont, "The Jesus Prayer Among the Monks of Egypt." *Eastern Churches Review,* 6 (1974): 66–71, dates this portion of the *Virtues* to the 7th or 8th century while Lucien Regnault, "Quelques apophthegmes arabes sur la 'Prière de Jésus,'" *Irénikon,* 52 (1979): 344–55, at 353–54, dates some apophthegms on the Jesus Prayer in the Arabic *Bustân al-ruhbân* (*The Garden of the Monks*) to the 6th or 7th century.

[28]Evelyn White's statement, 2.61, that the *Virtues* are "akin to and partly identical with the Apophthegmata" needs nuancing. The Coptic *Sayings* may be found in Am, 203–34 (chap. 1 below); the *Life* in Am, 46–117 (chap. 3 below).

[29]I am excluding #1, 32, and 73, which preserve a tiny portion of *AP* Macarius the Great 32 (= Coptic *Sayings* 22).

Intriguingly, two sayings from the Greek collection (20, 32) lie embedded in the *Virtues* like shards of pottery found in the fill of a monastic archeological site. *Apophthegmata* Macarius the Great 32 (= Coptic 22) reports that "they said of Abba Macarius the Great that he became, as it is written, a god upon earth."[30] *Virtues* 32 preserves this somewhat surprising belief in a parenthesis, while in *Virtues* 1 Macarius' guardian cherub (an important figure in the *Life*, mentioned twice in the *Virtues*) declares to Macarius that "Christ our God will make you god over this land on which will live a multitude of people."[31] *Apophthegmata* Macarius the Great 20 appears to be another shard, while *Virtues* 46–47 may preserve the pot entire. Saying 20 has Macarius declare, "If slander has become to you the same as praise, poverty as riches, deprivation as abundance, you will not die."[32] A parallel version of this declaration by Macarius occurs in *Virtues* 47, which is connected thematically to *Virtues* 46 by the term "reproach." *Virtues* 47 forms a coda and fitting conclusion to the long story in *Virtues* 46 of Macarius' exoneration and praise of a monk wrongly accused of theft who had accepted unjust rebuke with humiliation. Saying 20, preserved in the *Apophthegmata* without context (the "you" is not named), seems to be a snippet clipped off of a longer story, possibly preserved entire in *Virtues* 46–47.[33] Whatever the case here, it is clear that the *Virtues of Macarius* has connections with traditions found in both the *Sayings* and the *Life of Macarius of Scetis*; but it is also clear that the *Virtues* is not merely a slavish copy of those traditions but preserves a large body of material by (or at least attributed to) Macarius not found elsewhere. This alone makes it a very valuable addition to the canon of early monastic literature.

[30]Ward, 134.

[31]The parenthesis in #32 could be a scribal gloss.

[32]Ward, 131. There is one more sentence to the saying, not found in the *Virtues*.

[33]Saying 20 and *Virtues* 47 differ. In *Virtues* 47 Macarius orders an unnamed disciple, "Follow your conscience with your fellows and stay away from anyone who is arrogant," which seems to fit with the story in *Virtues* 46. Saying 20, by contrast, has a generalizing concluding moral ("Indeed, it is impossible for anyone . . ."), that seems to be an expansion of what is found in *Virtues* 47.

Another, not inconsiderable, value of the *Virtues of Saint Macarius* is that it preserves or restores, in part, the voice of Evagrius of Pontus (346–99), the great theologian and spiritual teacher of early monasticism. There can now be no doubt that in later monastic and patristic tradition Evagrius was either subsumed (Cassian), edited out (the *Apophthegmata*),[34] expropriated (the *Epistula fidei* passing down as Basil's *Epistle 8*), expurgated (the first Syriac version of the *Kephalaia Gnostica*), or disappeared (the Greek versions of many of his works). Recent scholarly studies have shown this process at work.[35] The *Virtues of Macarius*, by contrast, do not appear to know about the anti-Origenist opprobrium heaped posthumously upon Evagrius. In #69 he is given the epithet "Evagrius the wise" and in the collection he is placed in the company of such illustrious figures as Poemen, Paphnutius, and Moses.

Evagrius has six sayings attributed to him in the *Virtues*, just one less than the total assigned to him in the *Apophthegmata* (none of the sayings in the *Virtues* has a parallel in the *Apophthegmata*), and more than any other person in the *Virtues* except Macarius himself. The Evagrius that appears in the *Virtues* is a humble disciple seeking wisdom at the feet of his master, Macarius:[36] he inquires about "the purity of free will" (#17), asks for a saving word (#39), comes to Macarius distressed by his thoughts and the passions of the body (#42), asks how Satan throws evil thoughts at the brothers (#76), visits Macarius in the burning heat (#77),[37] and asks for the meaning of blasphemy against the Holy Spirit (#81). *Virtues* 39 is reminiscent of *Apophthegmata* Evagrius 7, where Evagrius is reminded that he is

[34] *Praktikos* 91 and 95 passed into the beginning of the *Systematic Apophthegmata* with Evagrius' name conspicuously absent; see Jean-Claude Guy, ed., *Les Apophtegmes des Pères*, 103–4.

[35] See BV and the Introduction to the companion volume to this one, *Four Desert Fathers*.

[36] On Macarius and Evagrius, see Gabriel Bunge, "Évagre le Pontique et les deux Macaires."

[37] *Virtues* 77, which may be found in essentially the same form in Evagrius, *Praktikos* 94, probably refers to Macarius of Alexandria and not Macarius of Egypt; see #77 and the note there.

no longer a great man in Constantinople but is now a humble seeker in the middle of nowhere. It has the echoing ring of desert truth:

> Abba Evagrius said, "I visited Abba Macarius and said to him, 'Tell me a word so I may live.'
>
> "He said to me, 'If I speak to you, will you listen and do it?'
>
> "I said to him, 'My faith and my love are not hidden from you.'
>
> "Abba Macarius said to me, 'Truly, I lack the adornment of virtue; you, however, are good. But if you cast off the pridefulness of this world's rhetoric and clothe yourself in the humility of the tax collector, you will live.'"

The Evagrius of the *Virtues* cannot automatically be assumed to be less authentic than the figure of Evagrius in the *Apophthegmata* or the *Lausiac History* of Palladius. In reconstructing a biography of Evagrius, one would have to give primary consideration to Palladius' account in the *Lausiac History*; even there, however, one senses a difference between the writings of Evagrius and Palladius' portrait of him, comparable to the differences between the writings of Augustine and Possidius' portrait of the bishop of Hippo. But there is no denying that Palladius offers an eyewitness portrait. Both the *Apophthegmata* and the *Virtues* were edited later, but both undoubtedly rely on earlier traditions. The *Virtues* report Evagrian traits that are unquestionably authentic. One notes in the *Virtues* Evagrius' interest in thoughts and the passions, two abiding concerns of his in his writings. In #39, Macarius chides Evagrius to "cast off the pridefulness of this world's rhetoric." Evagrius demonstrates notable rhetorical (and philosophical) expertise in his writings; such rhetorical polish, no doubt, looked prideful in the desert.[38] Whether the *Virtues* reports historical conversations between Evagrius and

[38]See *AP* Evagrius 7.

Macarius is impossible to say, but there is little doubt that these sayings come from the same tradition that remembered and collected the *Sayings of the Fathers*, a tradition that at some time and in some quarters highly valued Evagrius and his memory and passed fragments of that memory on as "saving words."

The historical questions surrounding the *Virtues of Saint Macarius* are interesting and important, but we should remember that the collection was compiled long ago not for historical but for ascetic and spiritual reasons. And it is as a spiritual work that the *Virtues* is compelling. The Macarius who appears here is not primarily a holy man or wonderworker (though he is both); instead, he is the "Spiritbearer" and teacher, a teller of parables. This Macarius is not unknown from other sources, but he comes to the forefront here. In *Apophthegmata* Macarius the Great 12 some fathers ask Macarius about his emaciation. He replies with a vivid metaphor: "The little bit of wood that is used to poke the vinebranches when they are burning ends by being entirely burnt up by the fire; in the same way, man purifies his soul in the fear of God, and the fear of God burns up his body."[39]

The saying just quoted is the only extended metaphor attributed to Macarius in the *Apophthegmata*; by contrast, the *Virtues* is filled with metaphor. And what vivid and lively images they are! To list just a few, Macarius uses as analogies a millstone, a mirror, a tunic and its patch, a child with a dirty diaper, a nursing mother, a ruminating sheep, a sheepfold, a potter, a ship's captain and ship's equipment, a smith's anvil, a goldsmith, a street vendor and his customer, a tree and its branches, an eagle, bees, beehives, flowers, and honey. Such use of metaphor and analogy was quite deliberate on Macarius' part: when a brother asks him (#11), "My father, how can a person be free from the passions and be renewed in the Spirit?", the old man said to him, "I will give you an analogy [-*ainigma*]." The tradition behind the *Virtues* understands that Macarius made frequent use of parable

[39]Ward, trans., 130.

(#43): "One time Abba Macarius told this parable when the brothers asked him about pity." If this tradition is correct, Macarius borrowed the use of parables from Jesus himself (#10, 21): "One time a brother asked Abba Macarius, 'Tell me, my father, what is it to throw oneself down before God?' Abba Macarius said to him, 'It is written that our Lord did not speak to people except in parables.' " In using parables, then, Macarius is imitating Jesus.

Unlike the Jesus of the parables (as opposed to the Jesus that the Gospels present explaining himself), the Macarius of the *Virtues* often explains himself at great length. The *Virtues* sometimes seem to reflect a later phase of monastic community and spirituality when disciples "began to find the process of consultation frustratingly obscure and inconclusive. Instead of welcoming the pregnant phrase, the brief exegesis, designed to feed their minds over a period of time, they sought for greater clarity, for more general rules of progress, for full and immediate explanation."[40] The *Virtues* as a whole are longer than the sayings in the *Apophthegmata*, although no general conclusion can be made from this: many of the *Virtues* are short and a number of apophthegmata attributed to Macarius are quite lengthy.[41] In the *Virtues*, however, disciples are constantly asking Macarius for explanations of his gnomic sayings: Poemen in 8, some brothers in 20–21, and a brother in 27–28. Even more tellingly, the *Virtues*, unlike the *Apophthegmata*, contains small treatises: 5, on the workings of the Paraclete; 18, on monastic virtues; and 68, on the anchoritic life. These treatises are more like passages from Cassian's *Conferences* than sayings or stories from the *Apophthegmata*. They represent developing monastic tradition; some of that tradition—how much, is impossible to say—undoubtedly goes back

[40]Philip Rousseau, "The Desert Fathers, Antony and Pachomius," in *The Study of Spirituality*, ed. Cheslyn Jones, et al. (London: SPCK, 1992), 119–30, at 121–22.

[41]See Graham Gould, *The Desert Fathers on Monastic Community* (Oxford: Clarendon, 1993), 18–25, who argues for the reliability and authenticity of longer narratives in the *Apophthegmata*. There are, Gould believes, 19, "good grounds for belief that the oral tradition could accurately pass on recollections, including narratives, about earlier figures."

to Macarius himself while some postdates him and relies on traditions about him.

What is the effect of the parables and extended stories in the *Virtues*? Like Jesus', they use the homely, the familiar, the everyday, to make striking spiritual observations and suggestions. Macarius, moreover, uses parables not just to strike a vivid image like a flint in the darkness, but to build a bonfire illuminating the mercy and compassion of Christ; he refers over and over again to Christ's "numerous treasuries of compassion," a compassion that comes from the incarnation and cross.[42] *Virtues* 38 offers a good example of both Macarius' method and his theology:

> Abba Macarius also said, "The potter who sits working the earth first takes care to fashion vessels decorated with colorful motifs that become honored at the morning and evening meals of emperors and are even honored by the priestly order of the Church. After making these, he fashions other vessels that are ugly and inferior for use as chamber pots and for birthing stools for the newborn and innocent. After making these, he loads the furnace and fires them. Truly I say that just as he prays for the precious and decorated vessels, he also prays for those that are ugly and inferior because they are works of his hand.
>
> "It is the same with our Lord Jesus Christ, who possesses the treasuries of numerous mercies, who alone is compassionate with his good Father and the Holy Spirit: just as he rejoices over the person who is honored and adorned with the pure progress of virtue and abstinence, he also rejoices over the conversion of someone who is inferior, that is, the sinner, as it is written, 'There will be rejoicing in heaven in the presence of the angels of God over one sinner, if he repents' [Lk 15:7]. He also said, 'I do not desire the death of

[42]The image of "treasuries" probably comes from Jesus: Mt 6:21, 13:44, 19:21.

the sinner so much as his conversion and his life' [See Ezek 33:11, 1 Tim 2:4 and 2 Pet 3:9]. When he took on this flesh, he also willingly accepted its griefs. On account of this, our Lord Jesus Christ also says, 'I have not come to invite the righteous to repentance but sinners' " [Mt 9:13].

The saying above is not an isolated example from the *Virtues*; they are suffused with its spirit, a spirit of humility, forgiveness, and compassion. The Macarius in these pages, whatever his relationship to the Macarius of history, is a wise and discerning spiritual father, one for whom judgment is a given, but also one for whom the incarnation has altered the very texture and shape of the cosmos.[43] Whatever the exact provenance and date of the *Virtues of Saint Macarius*, it offers some of the most powerful spiritual instruction not only in early monastic or early Christian literature but in all of Christian writing.

The Life of Saint Macarius of Scetis

Incubation; prophetic dreams and visions; visitations by Abraham, a cherub, an angel of the Lord, a divine voice, and the spirits of Saints Antony and Pachomius: these are some of the key figures and actions in the hagiographical *Life of Macarius of Scetis* attributed to Sarapion of Thmuis. The chief presence is Macarius the Great (300–390)—or, as the author of this *Life* says, not Macarius but the grace, power, and providence of God working through his saint. The *Life*, then, is not really a "life," interested in the quotidian events and occupations of one person's earthly existence; rather, "animated by

[43]James E. Goehring has noted that, because of the nature of the sources about them, the ancient monastic figures, like Jesus, are beyond the reach of history; see his *Ascetics, Society, and the Desert*, 13–35. I, however, believe that much of the historical Macarius survives in the sources; with regard to his compassion, see *AP* Macarius the Great 8, 15, and 21.

spiritual concerns and sustained by prayer," it is a theological and spiritual meditation on (one might say "assertion about") a saint and his importance as heavenly exemplar and godly mirror held up to the author's monastic audience (34).[44] Like most Coptic Lives, the *Life of Macarius of Scetis* may have originally been designed as a panegyric to be recited on the feast day of Saint Macarius.[45]

This *Life* should, first of all, be distinguished from the *Life of Macarius of Egypt*; the latter is part of the "Coptic Palladiana," one of four Coptic *Lives* with intriguing ties to the *Lausiac History* of Palladius (see the companion volume to this one, *Four Desert Fathers*).[46] The *Life of Macarius of Scetis* may be found in three tenth-century manuscripts from the Vatican Library,[47] and may have been written between 623 and 784.[48] Probably based on a Sahidic Coptic original, it is written in Bohairic Coptic with a smattering of Sahidic

---

[44]The quotation is from Columba Stewart's thoughtful review article, "Feature Review: Three Recent Studies on Ancient Monasticism" *American Benedictine Review*, 50.1 (1999), 3–11, 10. Numbers in parentheses refer to sections of the translation of the *Life* in Chapter Three below.

[45]Evelyn White, 2.111.

[46]See M. Chaîne, "La double recension de l'*Histoire Lausique* dans la version copte," *Revue de l'orient chrétien*, 25 (1925–26): 232–75, at 239–59, with additional textual material supplied by Adalbert de Vogüé, "La version copte du chapitre XVII de l'Histoire Lausiaque: Les deux éditeurs de les trois manuscrits," *Orientalia* 58.4 (1989): 510–24. On the "Coptic Palladiana," see Gabriel Bunge and Adalbert de Vogüé, *Quatre ermites égyptiens: Les fragments coptes de l'Histoire Lausiaque* (Spiritualité Orientale 60; Begrolles-en-Mauges: Bellefontaine, 1994). See now also Toda Satoshi, "La vie de S. Macaire l'Égyptien: État de la question," *Analecta Bollandiana*, 118:3–4 (2000): 267–90, who suggests, 286, that the "Long Recension" of the Coptic Palladiana may have a greater dependence on the *Life of Macarius of Scetis* than previously thought.

[47]Vatican Coptic codices LIX.6 (f. 96r-136v), LXII.1 (f. 1r–37v), and LXIV.1 (f. 1r–32v); the text was edited by E. Amélineau, with a French translation, "Vie de Macaire de Scété," *Histoire des moines de la Basse-Égypte*, 46–117. On the manuscripts, see Mark Sheridan, "Histoire Lausiaque 1141 [Book Review]," *Collectanea Cisterciensia*, 57.3 (1995): 548–52. On the date, see Sheridan, 550–51, and L.Th. Lefort, "Littérature bohaïrique," *Le Muséon*, 44 (1931): 115–35. Lefort shows that most Bohairic literary production dates to the ninth century and later, after the destruction of the library at the Monastery of Saint Macarius the Great.

[48]On the dating, see Antoine Guillaumont, "Christianismes orientaux," in *École Pratique des Hautes Etudes, Annuaire*, 76 (1968–1969): 182 (section V: Sciences religieuses).

spellings,[49] though it may have been composed originally in Greek.[50] Marginal notes show that the manuscript, like the *Virtues of Saint Macarius*, was used liturgically as a lectionary.[51]

The title page of the *Life of Macarius of Scetis* attributes the work to Sarapion of Thmuis, disciple of Saint Antony the Great and later bishop of the aforenamed city;[52] so literally right at the top of the page we are presented with historical difficulties: Sarapion purports to narrate the details of Macarius' death and burial; the bishop, however, died before 370, twenty years before Macarius' death.[53] It is like having Moses, as the author of the Pentateuch, narrate his own death at the end of Deuteronomy (34:5). Furthermore, the reading "Sarapion" is not assured. When Macarius pays his first visit to Antony (17), we are suddenly introduced to the narrator: "while he stayed there, he slept beside me each day—I, Sarapamōn, the most unworthy." Another codex (LIX) reads here "beside Sarapiōn, the old man's faithful disciple." These two spellings, however, may be interchangeable and thus may designate one person and not two people.[54]

---

[49]See, e.g., 55.10: *čloč*, "bed," for *čloj*; 93.15: *themko* (with an initial "theta"), "afflict, humiliate," for *themko* (with an initial "tau, hori"); 98.11: *telēl*, "rejoice, joy," for *thelēl*; 102.6: *čojčej*, "slice, hit, slaughter," for *čotčet, shoshet.*

[50]Toda, "La vie de S. Macaire," 268, has identified three recensions, A, B, and C, of which he identifies A as the oldest. He believes that the Coptic represents the earliest version but suggests also, 288, that "the primitive text of recension A circulated in Greek," indicated by a number of unusual Greek words in the Coptic text. Thus he concludes, 289, "if the original language was Greek, the Coptic would then have to be the translation of a lost Greek text." See 279–84 for his table comparing the Coptic, Syriac, and Greek versions. The Greek and Syriac versions, from recension C, are considerably longer than the Coptic version and contain material from the *Apophthegmata*, the *Lausiac History*, and the *Virtues of Macarius*. Toda has edited the Greek version for his mémoire de licence complémentaire at the Université catholique de Louvain and is working on a dissertation on the *Life of Macarius*. I wish to thank him for sending me an offprint of his article cited above.

[51]See notes 1, 140, and 142 of the *Life*. By "liturgically," I do not mean that it was necessarily used in church as part of the *synaxis* or eucharist, but that remains a possibility; it was probably used as part of *lectio divina* or the daily Office.

[52]Sheridan notes, 550–51, that Vat. LIX.6 and LXII.1 give Sarapion as the author, while LXIV.1, due to a mutilated beginning, lacks this identification but the attribution to Sarapion is nevertheless probable.

[53]See Evelyn White, 2.465.

[54]Evelyn White, 2.465 n. 4, argues this position and cites a superior of the

It is possible that the attribution to Sarapion *of Thmuis* is a pious mistake and that the *Life* was written or edited by another Sarapion who was a near-contemporary of Macarius, but the text presents further difficulties to this possibility.[55] Although presented as a disciple of Antony, Sarapion refers to "what we have heard from our fathers who preceded us" (2) and to "works of his that have been written in other books" (33), which suggest greater distance in time from his subject. A clue to proximate if not actual authorship may lie embedded in the text in a word the author uses at least seven times: *jom,* "power." When the cherub first speaks to Macarius, the heavenly being exhorts the saint, "Gird yourself with power from God, who gives you power" (15). In the next paragraph Sarapion makes it clear that Macarius was "guided by the cherub, or rather, by the power of God." Again, when Macarius heals the sick, it is "with a word from his mouth—or, rather, by the power of God" (24). Just as Macarius is given power by God, so too does it wane as he grows old and loses strength (*jom;* 29, 31, 33, 35), a point made by Sarapion four times.

Macarius, then, is a man of power, girded with and guided by the power of God.[56] Such an understanding (and incarnating) of divine power comes not from literature about Antony the Great but from works associated with or attributed to Macarius himself; specifically, from the *Virtues of Saint Macarius* 5 (conventionally titled *Ad filios Dei*), which in antiquity circulated independently of the *Virtues* as a

Monastery of John the Little who is called by both names. But such interchangeability is not normal in documentary texts (either Coptic or Greek); there are many variants of both names, but they do not seem to overlap. However, in certain hands they could conceivably be confused in the copying of a manuscript, which may have happened here. I wish to thank Terry Wilfong for his comments on this matter.

[55]As Evelyn White catalogues, 2.465–68 (Appendix III). Dom Butler posited another Sarapion as the author, a monk and contemporary of Macarius; see Evelyn White, 465 n. 7.

[56]A possible allusion to this understanding may be found in the *Virtues of Saint Macarius* 31 (Amélineau, *Histoire,* 148): "It was said about our father Saint Abba Macarius the Great that when he advanced in virtue he received power to intercede with our Lord Jesus Christ."

whole.[57] In *Ad filios Dei*, the term power occurs eight times, and early on is a "holy power" that God sends and withdraws. Eventually, though, it becomes clear that the Power equals the Paraclete which equals the Holy Spirit.[58] The Macarian tradition, in fact, seems to have associated this saint with the Holy Spirit in particular, calling him "the Spiritbearer."[59] This appellation appears less frequently in the earliest stratum of tradition, existing once in the Greek and Coptic sayings attributed to Macarius.[60] Macarius is called "Spiritbearer" once in the main body of the *Virtues of Saint Macarius*.[61] In what serves as the work's coda, however, Abba Poemen emphasizes that Macarius was indeed the bearer of the Spirit:

> Abba Poemen said, "Every time I met Abba Macarius I did not say a single word without him already having knowledge of it because he was a Spiritbearer and possessed a prophetic spirit, like Elijah and all the other prophets, for he was clothed with humility like a cloak through the power of the Paraclete who dwelt in him. He alone possessed foresight and was filled with the grace of God; the glory of the Lord shone on his face; the consolation of the Consoler, the Holy

[57]For the Coptic text, see Amélineau, *Histoire*, 122–25; for a translation and discussion, see Tim Vivian, "The Good God, the Holy Power, and the Paraclete: 'To the Sons of God' (*Ad filios Dei*) by Saint Macarius the Great," *Anglican Theological Review*, 30.3 (1998): 338–65.

[58]See Vivian, ibid., pars. 9–11, 13–15, pp. 363–64.

[59]The title page to the *Life* refers to Macarius this way, but it also apples the same epithet to Antony the Great. The term "Spiritbearer" (*pneumatophoros*) goes back to the hermetic writings and is also found in the Old Testament (LXX): Hos 9:7 and Zeph [Sophonias] 3:4. Its first use in the Christian tradition is in *The Shepherd of Hermas*, Mandate 11:16. *AP* Antony the Great 30 applies it to Saint Antony, *LH* 11.5 to Evagrius, and the *Life of John the Little* 58 and 64 to John Kolobos. On the development of the idea of Spiritbearer, see Peter Nagel, *Die Motivierung der Askese in der alten Kirche und der Ursprung des Mönchtums* (TU 95; Berling: Akademie-Verlag, 1966), 69–75.

[60]*AP* Macarius the Great 38 (PG 65.280A) = Coptic *Sayings* 30 (Amélineau, *Histoire*, 225).

[61]*Virtues* 69; Amélineau, 185. The *Life of John the Little* 82 applies the term to Macarius.

Spirit, which was with him, came down upon everyone sitting around him.[62]

The repeated use of "power" in the *Life*; its significance in *Ad filios Dei*, a work which is attributed to Macarius; the equation of power (or: Power) in *Ad filios Dei* with the Holy Spirit; and the naming of Macarius as "the Spiritbearer" in the *Virtues of Saint Macarius* and his close association with the Paraclete and Holy Spirit all suggest that the *Life* was composed or edited not by a disciple of Antony the Great (Sarapion of Thmuis) but by someone from a community that especially venerated Saint Macarius the Great and was acutely conscious of his divine power.

Whoever the author or editor was, it is clear that he had access to early oral or written material about Macarius (the "other books" that he mentions). What is striking is how diverse these sources are: in addition to allusions to the *Life of Antony* (discussed below), there are parallels with the Greek *Apophthegmata Patrum*, the Coptic *Sayings of Saint Macarius*, the *Virtues of Macarius*, and the *Life of Macarius of Egypt* ("Coptic Palladiana"). Here is a synoptic view of the parallels:

8. "Macarius the Camel-driver": *AP* Macarius 31; Coptic *Sayings* 12.
14. Girl Accuses Macarius of Impregnating Her: *AP* Macarius 1; *Sayings* 1
15, 16, 18, 22, 27. The Cherub: *Virtues* 1, 73.
17, 19. Antony: *AP* Macarius 4, 26
21. The Two Young Romans: *AP* Macarius 33; Coptic *Sayings* 8.
28. The Men on the Island: *AP* Macarius 2; Coptic *Sayings* 21.
32. The Healing of Agathonicus' Daughter: *AP* Macarius 7; *Virtues* 3.

[62] *Virtues* 83; Amélineau, 202.

33. Written in Other Books: *Life of Macarius of Egypt* 11.

33. The Faithful Women: Coptic *Sayings* 33.

34. Macarius Like God: *AP* Macarius 32; Coptic *Sayings* 22;
   Virtues 1, 32.

36. Paphnutius: *AP* Macarius 28, 37; *Sayings* 3, 15; *Virtues* 17,
   65, 74.

With these parallels, it is better to say that the *Life of Macarius of Scetis* was edited rather than written, perhaps by a Sarapion, more assuredly by someone in a "Macarian" community who had access to other works or oral traditions about the saint.

But what are we to make of the passages that have no parallels elsewhere, especially the material about Macarius' early life? Conflicts arise here between the *Life* and other sources. According to the *Life* (19), Macarius began to gather disciples only after his second visit to Antony and Antony's death in 356, but *Apophthegmata* Macarius 26 has Macarius, on a visit to Antony, reveal that there are already numerous "fathers" with him in Scetis.[63] The *Life* clearly states (13, 14) that Macarius was a priest before he went to Scetis: when a young village girl becomes pregnant by her relative, the two meet and say to one another, "What will we do? If our parents find out about it they will kill us, but let's say that the priest, the anchorite, is the one who did it because he's a stranger and no mercy will be shown to him" (14). The much shorter version of this story in the *Apophthegmata*, however, and its Coptic parallel, say only "the anchorite," and not "the priest."[64] More dramatically, the author of

[63] See also *AP* Amoun 3; Evelyn White, 2.66.

[64] *AP* Macarius the Great 1 (= Coptic *Sayings* 1). This same saying, in both Greek and Coptic, says that villagers "seized me and made me a cleric for the village." However, both versions then report that Macarius did not wish this honor so he fled. Given this context, Ward translates "they took me to make me a cleric in the village" (Ward, 124). See PG 65.257 and Amélineau, *Histoire*, 203. Palladius does not clarify matters much. *LH* 17.2 says that by the time Macarius was forty he had "received the gift of healing spirits and of prophecy. He was even [*de kai*] deemed worthy of the priesthood"; *Palladio: La Storia Lausiaca*, ed. G. J. M. Bartelink (Milan: Fondazione Lorenzo Valla, 1974), 70. Evelyn White, 63, 66, 466, argues that Macarius was ordained priest ten years

the *Life* is so intent on making Macarius the follower and heir of Antony that, in opposition to other early sources, he makes him one of the two disciples who buried the great saint.[65] Finally, according to the *Life*, Macarius dies at ninety-seven, weak, but still fighting the Devil, while Palladius (*LH* 17.2) says that he died at the age of ninety.[66] None of these in itself decisively shows that the *Life* is ahistorical while the other early sources are historically accurate.[67] The discrepancies do warrant historical caution, however, especially when coupled with the author's hagiographical intentions (discussed at the end of this Introduction), purposes which were not, after all, historical.

There are, unfortunately, no firm dates to be gleaned from the *Life*, only inferential ones.[68] Sarapion refers to the founding, under Macarius' tutelage, of three other monasteries in Scetis: Baramus (the Monastery of the Romans), John the Little, and Bishoi. All three have their founding in the mid- to late-fourth century, but the story surrounding Baramus is the most intriguing.[69] As told in the *Apoph-*

---

after going to Scetis (having gone there, by his reckoning, in 330 at the age of thirty), but Palladius does not specifically say that Macarius was also a priest by the time he was forty. Evelyn White also adduces *AP* Macarius 2, which again is ambiguous.

[65]Thus confusing Macarius of Jijbēr with Macarius of Pispir; see Evelyn White, 2.466. The *Life of Antony* 91.1, 92.2 leaves the two disciples unnamed, while Jerome, *Life of Paul, the First Hermit* 1, gives their names as Amathas and Macarius; see Paul B. Harvey, Jr., trans., "Jerome: Life of Paul, the First Hermit," in Vincent L. Wimbush, ed., *Ascetic Behavior in Greco-Roman Antiquity: A Sourcebook* (Minneapolis: Fortress, 1990), 357–69; 360.

[66]Evelyn White thus believes, 2.466, that the *Life* has conflated the final days of Macarius of Egypt with those of Macarius of Alexandria. On this problem, see Antoine Guillaumont, "Le problème des deux Macaires" and Gabriel Bunge, "Évagre le Pontique et les deux Macaires."

[67]Even Evelyn White, who does not think highly of the *Life* as a historical source, acknowledges that portions probably rely on early traditions; see 2.60–72, 465–68. To give just one example, the removal of Macarius' remains from Scetis to Jijbēr (37) does not seem like something that a hagiographer or tradition was likely to invent.

[68]If the "soldiers" in 16 refer to Moses the Black and his disciples, then the date of their martyrdom is 407–8; see the note at 16.

[69]On the dates of the Monastery of John the Little and Monastery of Saint Bishoi, see Evelyn White, 2. 110 and 113, and on Baramus, 98–103.

thegmata, or *Sayings of the Desert Fathers* (Macarius the Great 33),
two young "strangers" came to Scetis, lived edifying lives, and died
young. They so impressed Macarius that "when the Fathers came to
see" him, "he used to take them to their cell, and say, 'Come and see
the *martyrion* of the young strangers.'"[70] The Coptic *Sayings* preserves this story in essentially the same form.[71] In the *Life* the two
young foreigners come "from parts of the Roman Empire," and after
their deaths "were buried beside the cave [where they had lived] and
. . . the whole area came to be called the laura of the Romans and is
called that to this day" (21). The two strangers remain unnamed, but
they are now Romans, and their cave has been transformed from a
shrine (*martyrion*) to a laura, a monastic community of semi-
anchorites. The story continued to grow. Evelyn White has summa-
rized its development:

> In the late fifth or early sixth century these saints were con-
> fused with the royal pupils of the Roman Arsenius, emerg-
> ing as Roman princes who (to evade awkward historical
> facts) were identified as sons of Valentinian I [364–75]. At
> about the same time, or possibly later, the story of the north-
> Palestinian Maximus and Domitius (probably real persons)
> was absorbed into the growing legend, with the result that
> the nameless youths who joined Macarius, now duly
> equipped with names and rank, stood forth as "Our Fathers
> the Romans, Maximus and Domitius," patron saints though
> not truly originators of the Monastery of Baramûs.[72]

Evelyn White believes that the identification of the two as Romans
occurred after 444 but that the real development of the story took
place after 451 and had become stereotyped by 600.[73] Since the two

[70]PG 65.277B.
[71]Coptic *Sayings* 8; Amélineau, 211.
[72]Evelyn White, 2.102–3.
[73]Evelyn White, 2.103. He notes that Maximus and Domitius are "Monophysite"
saints only and do not appear in the calendars of Chacedonian Churches.

are unnamed in the *Life*, it is reasonable to place its version toward the beginning of this timeline, in the mid-fifth century.

A striking event in the *Life*, the "theft" of Macarius' remains, provides a *terminus ante quem* for the work. Sometime after the monks of Scetis had "placed his holy body in the cave beside the church that he had built and went to their dwellings in great mourning" (36), the people of Jijbēr "found out where the saint's body had been laid (Jijbēr was the saint's village, as we made clear at the beginning of the narrative) and they came down to Scetis secretly, without anyone knowing about them, and they took the body of our blessed father to their village." There they "made a great casket of costly wood," "placed his holy body in it," "built a *martyrion* southwest of the village," and "sent for the holy bishop . . . and asked him to consecrate the building." This pious theft must have occurred around 390. Macarius' relics were removed again, to Elmi, in 784, and so the *Life* was written or edited before this second removal.[74] Since the *Life* preserves an intermediate version of the legend of Maximus and Domitius, and since it is devoid of any anti-Chalcedonian polemic, it seems reasonable to suggest a date of around 450 for its composition (or, better: construction).

"What is written," Sarapion declares at the beginning of the *Life*, "looks toward a single end, the incarnation of our Savior . . . who was crucified for us and endured death in the flesh in order to save us and the whole world from the grasp of the Devil" (1). The world for Sarapion is still very much in Satan's grasp, but Saint Abba Macarius, "our righteous father," "an apostle for his time,"[75] "broke and destroyed all of the Enemy's powerful weapons and scattered his armor" (38). Over and again Sarapion asserts that Macarius had the power (*jom*) of God in him and was guided by the Holy Spirit. Therefore any history of Macarius will be salvation history, and so in his proemium Sarapion looks back to Holy Scripture for guidance in understanding the blessed (*makarios*) saint.

[74]Evelyn White, 468.
[75]A textual variant has "for our time."

Macarius is a "promised child" and his parents, we are to understand, are like Abraham and Sarah. Abraham, in fact, appears to Macarius' father and delivers this prophecy:

> Do not be afraid. I am Abraham, the father of Isaac who begot Jacob. Therefore, listen to me. Do not disobey the voice of your wife. Leave this land, for God has so decided it. Come, live in Jijbēr. "I will not forsake you," says the Lord, "but I will bless you," he said, for I too left my country of Haran and I dwelt in the land of Canaan, as the Lord told me: "And I will give you a son," said the Lord, "from this wife whom you now have, and his name will endure for generations with the children that he will beget spiritually to serve me in the place that I will show him." (3)

This promise is fulfilled both then and in the future: an "angel of the Lord" later appears to Macarius' father (as to Zechariah and Joseph in the Gospels), heals him of an illness, and tells him to "know" his wife; Macarius' mother conceives and bears a son, just as the angel has promised. Later, when he is grown, a man dressed "in a garment that cast forth lightning and was multi-colored and striped" appears to Macarius and declares, "Thus says God: 'This land I will give to you. You shall dwell in it and blossom and your fruits shall increase and your seed shall multiply and you shall bear multitudes of spiritual children and rulers who will suckle at your breasts'" (8). Macarius is thus both Abraham and Moses (and lactating Madonna?), chosen by God to bear spiritual offspring and lead them to the promised land of salvation.

For this awesome task the Lord appoints a cherub, who appears to Macarius and spurs him to action while reinforcing both the divine promise and God's protection:

> Do not be afraid of anything: the Lord has commanded me not only to tell you to leave here but also to be with you in the

place the Lord has shown you until what you have heard spoken to you is fulfilled. For God has decided to make you the father of a multitude, not through fleshly generation, but by the calling of spiritual children. I have been ordered by God to serve the people that you will gather together in accordance with the decision of my God; I will serve them in secret until the end of days—if, of course, they keep the precepts and commandments of the Lord that you will give them (15).

Heavenly direction also requires earthly counsel, and so Macarius goes to visit Antony the Great. This is Sarapion's second major hagiographical theme: making Macarius the spiritual child of Antony, as the numerous allusions in the work to the *Life of Antony* demonstrate.[76] Macarius, besieged by demons and doubts, goes to Antony for instruction on how to live in the desert; Macarius asks to stay, but Antony refuses (17). He returns to Scetis and later, while the demons continued "to fight against him by means of these thoughts, he got up and went to Saint Antony," who comforts and encourages him again and tells him that he has "been called to be the father of many nations who will love the true philosophy of monasticism." Antony later "clothed Abba Macarius in the monastic habit and," Sarapion emphasizes, "this is the reason he is called the disciple of Abba Antony." After Antony dies, Macarius helps Sarapion bury him and returns to Scetis (19). It is only then, undoubtedly contrary to historical fact, that Macarius begins to call disciples. In the *Life of Antony* 91.8–9, Athanasius has Antony pass the mantle, both literally and figuratively, to two bishops, Sarapion and Athanasius himself. In the *Life of Macarius*, by contrast, "Sarapion" (who is not Bishop Sarapion of Thmuis) has Antony give his walking stick and pass his spiritual fatherhood on to the monk Macarius.[77] Sarapion will later

[76]See 9, 11, 12, 16, and the references there. More generally, both the *Life of Macarius* and the *Life of Antony* share the view that their saints are under pervasive assault by demons.

[77]It seems doubtful that a devoted follower of Antony would have Antony's fatherhood pass to a monk of Scetis (even to *the* monk of Scetis) rather than to one

carefully note that Paphnutius in turn "assumed the fatherhood in the holy places after Abba Macarius, for he too was a holy man and had pursued the same course as the holy man Abba Macarius the Great" (36). Thus Sarapion establishes two lineages, one heavenly (or divine): God to Abraham to Macarius; and one earthly and monastic (or human): Antony to Macarius to Paphnutius.

These two realms unite at Macarius' death when the two great founders of anchoritic and cenobitic monasticism, Antony and Pachomius respectively, visit Macarius. Just as Abraham and the cherub had earlier told Macarius to "go live in the place that was shown to you once by our Lord" (15), Antony now prophesies to the old man that "in another nine days you will lay aside the garment of skin and you will dwell with us. Lift your eyes to heaven and see the place that has been prepared for you in order for you to rejoice and enter into rest" (34). After the saints withdraw from him,

little by little, he lost his strength [*jom*]. On the night when his illness was moving from the eighth to the ninth day, as Abba Antony had said . . . suddenly that cherub, who had remained with him from the beginning, came with large multitudes of incorporeal choirs and said to him, "Hurry, come, for all those standing around you will testify on your behalf." And Abba Macarius said in a loud voice, "Lord Jesus, my soul's beloved, receive my spirit!" And so he went to sleep (35).

For the believer, of course, Macarius' death is the beginning of life eternal. For Sarapion, as proclaimer of the "word" of Macarius through his *Life*, the saint's life marks the beginning point for his listeners as he urges them forward on the road of monastic emulation: "learn from this partial account what sort of life this man lived who was perfect in righteousness":

of Antony's own disciples at Pispir: one more reason to question the authorship of Sarapion of Thmuis, the disciple of Antony.

Therefore, when we hear these things, my beloved, let each of us evince in himself this same zeal for perfecting this kind of faith until the end as we behold today the way of life of this perfect man—I am speaking about our blessed father. Let us bear for God the fruits of the Spirit, like those we have seen in his admirable life (keeping, like painters, their images before our eyes at all times), and with these images in mind let us produce fruits that are fitting for the godly life to which Christ our God has called us through both the advocacy of our holy father and his teaching (38).

This, then, is the purpose of the *Life*: not to write history, but to rewrite the soul. Sarapion wants to hold Macarius up as a mirror to his monastic charges, but not simply as a mirror that gives the monk back only his own reflection; this mirror, imbued with Macarius' image (*icon*), can, Sarapion believes, through the grace and power of God, so change and transform the believer that he becomes the image and likeness of Macarius: "After God all of them looked at him as though looking in a mirror and their souls grew strong through his encouragement" (34). And Macarius, as Sarapion, has just pointed out (34), "was like God." Thus transformed, the emulator, in Sarapion's soteriology of place (the desert as saving place is the gateway and path to heaven, the place of eternal salvation), will be eligible to "be reconciled with him in the places that he has prepared for us in the everlasting kingdom of heaven, those places that are prepared for us with him" (38).

CHAPTER ONE

The Sayings of Saint Macarius of Egypt

SYNOPTIC TABLE

Comparing the Coptic Sayings *of Macarius with the Greek Alphabetical and Systematic* Apophthegmata Patrum[1]

Coptic Sayings	Greek Alph.[2]	Greek Sys.[3]
1. Abba Macarius Tells Why He Came to Scetis	1 (Ward, 124–25)[4]	XV.39
2. Abba Macarius Speaks about God's Consuming Fire	12 (Ward, 130)	III.18
3. Abba Macarius Still Weeps over a Youthful Sin	37 (Ward, 136)	
4. The Decline of Scetis	25 (Ward, 133)	
5. Abba Macarius' Rule about Drinking Wine	10 (Ward, 129)	IV.29
6. The Devil Is Powerless against Abba Macarius	11 (Ward, 129–30)	XV.40
7. Abba Macarius Heals Agathonicus' Daughter[5]		
8. The Story of the Two Young Foreigners	33 (Ward, 134–36)	XX.3

---

[1]Many of the cross-references in this table are from Lucien Regnault, *Les Sentences des Pères du désert: Troisieme recueil et tables* (Solesmes, 1976), 151–191.

[2]The references are first to the numbered sayings in the chapter on Saint Macarius in the alphabetical Greek collection of the Alphabetical *Apophthegmata Patrum* (*AP*) found in PG 65.257–82 and, in parentheses, to the page numbers of the English translation by Ward, 124–38. Titles are my own.

[3]The Greek Systematic Sayings may be found in Jean-Claude Guy, ed., *Les Apophtegmes des pères: Collection systématique. Chapitres I-IX* (SC 387; Paris: Cerf, 1993).

[4]A much longer version of this story occurs in the *Life of Macarius of Scetis* 14.

[5]This story can be found in the *Life of Macarius of Scetis* 32 (Am, 101–5) and *Virtues of Saint Macarius* 3 (Am, 120).

[6]This saying occurs as Anonymous *Apophthegmata Patrum* *J 671 Poemen (Regnault #1671).

[7]See also *Virtues of Saint Macarius* 1, 32, and 74.

[8]See *Virtues of Saint Macarius* 45.

[9]This saying occurs as Anonymous *Apophthegmata Patrum* N 16 Macarius (Regnault #1016).

CONCERNING ABBA MACARIUS THE GREAT[11]

Abba Macarius Tells Why He Came to Scetis (Macarius 1; Ward, 124–25)[12]

1   [203] Abba Macarius *once* spoke about himself, saying, "When I was a young man I lived in a cell in Egypt. I was seized and made a

[10]Although this saying (story, really) is not found in the Greek Alphabetical Collection, it is found in the Greek Systematic Collection XX.21. It is also found in the *Vitae Patrum* III.97 (PL 73.778; repr. from the Latin Collection of Pseudo-Rufino, *Vitae Patrum*, Liber III, interprete Pseudo-Rufino, ed. Heribert Rosweyde, *Vitae Patrum* III [Antwerp: Plantin, 1615]) and *Vitae Patrum* VI [XX.17] (PL 73.1013–14; repr. from Heribert Roswedye, ed. *Verba Seniorum* of Pelagius and John [Antwerp: Plantin, 1615 (and Lyons, 1617; rev. ed., 1628)]). An English translation of the latter may be found in Owen Chadwick, ed., *Western Asceticism* (Library of Christian Classics; Philadelphia: Westminster, 1958), 188. This saying is numbered by Nau as 489 (= Regnault 1489); see Lucien Regnault, *Les Chemins de Dieu au Désert: Collection Systematique des Apophtegmes des Pères* (Solesmes: Éditions de Solesmes, 1992), 170. See also Jean-Claude Guy, *Recherches sur la tradition grecque des Apophthegmata Patrum* (Subsidia Hagiographica, 36; Brussels: 1962, rev. ed., 1984), 176 (XX.21).

[11]Translated from Vat. copt. 64, 113f-152r and 59, 137f-153f, edited by E. Amélineau, *Histoire*, 203–34. Numbers in brackets indicate the pagination of Amélineau's text. Titles are the translator's. References following the titles are to the Alphabetical Collection of the *Apophthegmata Patrum* and to Benedicta Ward's translation. Portions in italics do not occur in the Greek Alphabetical collection (see n. 2); sayings in italics likewise are not found in that collection, although some do occur elsewhere (see the table above). The top of the MS. reads "The fourth Sunday of Lent," apparently a rubric stating when these sayings were read in the Church calendar.

[12]This story also appears in the *Life of Macarius of Scetis* 14.

cleric for the village[13] and, since I did not want this to happen, I fled to another place. A God-fearing lay person came to me;[14] he took my manual work and served me. Because of temptation, a young woman from the village fell and became pregnant. She was asked, 'Who did this to you?' and she said, 'The anchorite.' And so the people left the village and seized me and brought me to the village; they hung basket handles on me and different kinds of pots smeared with soot and led me through the village, beating me in every street, saying, [204] 'This monk has defiled our daughter,'[15] and they beat me almost to death.[16]

"An old man came and said to them, 'How long are you going to kill this venerable[17] monk?' The man who served me was walking behind me shamefacedly, for they were heaping abuse on him, saying, 'Look at this anchorite on whose behalf you've testified! Look what he's done!' And her parents said, 'Don't let him go until he guarantees that he will take care of her!' I spoke to my servant, who vouched for me, and I went to my cell. I gave him all the baskets I had on hand, saying, 'Sell them and give my wife something to eat.' And I said to myself, 'Macarius, look, you have found yourself a wife: you have to work a little harder in order to take care of her.' So I worked night and day and sent my work to her.

"When the time came for the wretched girl to give birth, she was in labor many days and did not give birth. They said to her, 'What's the matter?' and she said, 'I know that I am the cause of this; I treated

[13]This is noteworthy for two reasons. First, Macarius' cell was near a village and thus he was a village ascetic at that time; second, the chronology coincides with the Coptic *Life of Macarius of Scetis* 13, 14, that Macarius was ordained *before* he went to Scetis. (It is not clear here, however, whether Macarius was ordained and then fled or whether he fled before he was ordained.) Evelyn White, 2.63, 66, 466, argues that Macarius was ordained priest ten years *after* his withdrawal to Scetis.

[14]John the Little also had "a devout layman" to serve him at Klysma; see Maged S. Mikhail and Tim Vivian, "Life of Saint John the Little," *Coptic Church Review*, 18.1–2 (1997): 3–64, at 51.

[15]Gk: virgin; or: young woman (*parthenon*). Coptic lacks: catch him, catch him.

[16]Basket handles would make it possible for people to hang bells and, perhaps, pots and pans from them. Thus as the person moved he would make a lot of noise.

[17]Literally "old." Gk: foreign.

the anchorite unjustly and falsely slandered [205] him. This is not his doing but that of a certain young man; *he got me pregnant.*' The man who served me came from the village rejoicing and said, 'The young woman was unable to give birth until she confessed, saying, "This is not the work of the anchorite: I lied about him." What's more, the whole village wants to come and honor you and ask your forgiveness.' But when I heard this, and so people would not be able to bother me, I got up and fled and came here to Scetis. This is what first caused me to come here."

Abba Macarius Speaks about God's Consuming Fire (Macarius 12; Ward, 130)

2   Some old men[18] questioned Abba Macarius the Egyptian, "Whether you eat or whether you fast, your body is dried up."[19]

The old man said to them, "Fire insatiably consumes the wood that is employed for kindling for the fire; likewise, if a person purifies his heart in the fear of God, the fear of God consumes his bones."[20]

Abba Macarius Still Weeps over a Youthful Sin (Macarius 37; Ward, 136)

3   Abba Paphnutius, the disciple of Abba Macarius, said, "The old man said, 'When I was a boy, I used to pasture cattle with some other [206] boys.[21] They went to gather cucumbers[22] and they dropped one of them. When I picked it up, I ate it. Whenever I remember this, I sit down and weep.' "

[18]Gk: fathers.
[19]A desirable monastic trait, since dryness staved off "wet" sexual impulses.
[20]Gk: body.
[21]Ward mistakenly translates "I used to eat bilberries."
[22]Gk: figs.

The Decline of Scetis (Macarius 25; Ward, 133)

4   Abba Poemen begged the forgiveness of Abba Macarius many times[23] and said, "Tell me a word,"[24] and when the old man spoke, he said to him, "What you seek has now disappeared from among the monks."

Abba Macarius' Rule about Drinking Wine (Macarius 10; Ward, 129)

5   It was said about Abba Macarius the Egyptian that if he happened upon some brothers *who were eating,* he imposed a rule upon himself:[25] if there was wine,[26] in exchange for drinking a cup, he would spend a day without drinking water. So the brothers, for the sake of refreshment, would give wine to him and the old man would joyfully accept it in order to humble himself. But when his disciple discovered what was happening, he said to them, "For God's sake, do not give him any more wine. Isn't it enough that he punishes himself in his cell?" When the brothers understood what harm they were doing, they did not offer him wine.

The Devil Is Powerless against Abba Macarius (Macarius 11; Ward, 129–30)[27]

6   One time Abba Macarius was passing through the wadi to his cell carrying some palm leaves. The Devil met him on the road with a scythe. He attempted to strike Abba Macarius but was not able to.

---

[23]Gk: with many tears.

[24]Coptic lacks: how may I be saved?

[25]Gk uses the imperative form of the verbs, as though Macarius were speaking to himself, so Ward has placed Macarius' "rule" in quotation marks.

[26]Coptic lacks: for the brothers' sake.

[27]This saying occurs in the *Virtues of Saint Macarius* 2.

He said to Abba Macarius, "You are very powerful, Macarius! I am unable to do anything [207] against you. Look! Whatever you do, I also do: you fast, and I do not eat at all; you keep vigil, and I do not sleep at all. In one thing alone are you victorious over me."

Abba Macarius said to him, "What is that?"

He said, "Your humility. Because of your humility I am unable to do anything against you."[28]

When Abba Macarius spread out his hands, the demon disappeared.

Abba Macarius Heals Agathonicus' Daughter[29]

7   *It was said about Abba Macarius that when Agathonicus, the procurator[30] of Antioch, heard that he had these great powers and these gifts[31] of healing through our Lord Jesus Christ, he sent him his daughter, who had an unclean spirit, so he could pray over her. Through the grace[32] of God that was in him, when he prayed over her she was immediately healed and he sent her in peace to her parents. When her father and her mother saw the healing that Christ had accomplished for their daughter through the prayers and intercessions of the holy old man Abba Macarius, they gave thanks[33] to our Lord Jesus Christ.*

---

[28]For a very similar saying, see *AP* Theodora 6 (Ward, 84).

[29]This story occurs in the *Virtues of Saint Macarius* 3 and the *Life of Macarius of Scetis* 32.

[30]Procurators were agents of the emperor in the civil administration and were posted to minor provinces such as Judea.

[31]Or "graces," *hmot.*

[32]*Hmot.*

[33]*Aushep hmot.*

The Story of the Two Young Foreigners (Macarius 33; Ward,
134–36)[34]

8   Abba Pijimi[35] said, "*Abba Macarius' disciple told me this, saying,*
'The old man told me one time, "When I was sitting [208] in my
dwelling in Scetis, two young men, *foreigners and* strangers, came to
see me; one had a beard while the other one had just begun one.
They came to me and said, 'Where is Abba Macarius' cell?' I said to
them, 'What do you want with him?' They said to me, 'When we
heard about his works and about Scetis, we came to see him.' I said
to them, 'I am he.' They begged my pardon and said, 'We want to live
here.' I saw that they were soft and had been raised in luxury. I said
to them, 'You're not able to live here.' The older one said, 'If we can
not live here, we will go somewhere else.' I thought to myself, 'Why
should I run them off and be a stumbling block to them?'[36] I said to
them, 'Come, you two, build a cell for yourselves, if you can.' They
said, 'Just show us how and we will make one.'

"'"I gave them a pickaxe and a spade and a bag with bread and
salt. I showed them the rock of an abandoned quarry and said to
them, 'Cut yourselves a place here and bring some wood for yourselves from the wadi, make a roof, and thus you can live here.' I
thought that on account of the hardship they would flee in a hurry.
They asked me, 'What kind of work is done here?' I said to them,
'Plaiting,' and I got some palm leaves from the wadi. I showed them
[209] the rudiments of plaiting and how to weave. I said to them,
'Make baskets, give them to the guardians,[37] and they will bring you
bread.' Then I went away.

[34]On the historical and legendary aspects of these two monks, named elsewhere
as Maximus and Domitius, and the founding of the Monastery of the Romans (Pa
Romeos or Baramus), see Evelyn White, 2.98–104; for the expanded story, see the Coptic *Life of Maximus and Domitius*, Amélineau, *Histoire*, 262ff.

[35]Gk: Bitimios. The Gk has Bitimios saying that the story comes directly from
Macarius.

[36]Coptic lacks: Suffering will make them go away of their own accord.

[37]Or "watchmen," *ourati*, Gk *tois phulaxi*; see Crum, 738a, s.v. *hourit*. These
guardians also functioned at Nitria. On the interplay between work and food, see

" ' "They, however, patiently did everything I had ordered them and they did not come to see me for three years. I for my part wrestled with my thoughts, thinking, 'What is their way of life? They haven't come to see me about their thoughts.[38] Those who live far away come to see me but these two do not come, nor have they gone to anyone else, only to church, and only to receive the eucharist, keeping silent all the while.' I prayed to God and fasted for a week so he would show me their way of life. I got up and went to visit them in order to see how they were living.

" ' "When I knocked, one of them opened the door for me and they greeted me in silence. After we prayed, we sat down. The older one made a sign to the younger one, who left, and he remained sitting in silence, working at his plaiting. He did not say a word. When he knocked [210] at the ninth hour,[39] the younger one came in and when the older one made a sign to him he[40] laid a small mat and when the older one signaled to him he set down three loaves of bread[41] and stood in silence. I said, 'Let us rise and eat,' and we got up and ate and they brought a small pitcher and we drank.

Bentley Layton, "Social Structure and Food Consumption in an Early Christian Monastery: The Evidence of Shenoute's Canons and the White Monastery Federation A.D. 385–465," *Le Muséon*, 115.1–2 (2002): 25–57. "Guardians" may have been stewards of breadstores. The Arabic cited by Crum has a somewhat different meaning: "The carriers who carry the natron." The Arabic "carriers" or "haulers" designates a person whose work is to haul or carry a product, "workers" or "laborers" to be more generic. I wish to thank Maged Mikhail for his advice on the Arabic.

[38]The giving of spiritual counsel (usually by an elder to a younger monk) is extremely important in early monasticism: in the *Apophthegmata Patrum*, Abba Paphnutius reports that he went to see elders twice a month, walking some 12 miles (*AP* Paphnutius 3; PG 65:380), and Abba John the Little used to sit in front of the church on weekends so that monks might approach him about their thoughts (*AP* John Colobos 8; PG 65:205). See also Tim Vivian, "Words to Live By: 'A Conversation that the Elders Had with One Another Concerning Thoughts (ΠΕΡΙ ΛΟΓΙΣΜΩΝ),'" *St. Vladimir's Theological Quarterly*, 39:2 (1995): 127–41, and Columba Stewart, "Radical Honesty about the Self: the Practice of the Desert Fathers," *Sobornost*, 12 (1990): 25–39. Failure to seek counsel could lead to presumptuous self-importance and ruin; see *LH* 27.2.

[39]About three p.m., the normal time for eating if the monk ate only one meal a day.
[40]Coptic lacks: made a little soup and.
[41]Three loaves is often cited (e.g., *Life of Symeon the Holy Fool* 49 [PG

" ' "When evening came they said to me, 'Are you leaving?' I said, 'No, I will sleep here,' and they placed a mat for me to one side and they slept on the other side. They took off their cinctures and their scapulars and lay down in my presence.[42] I prayed to God to reveal to me their way of life. The roof opened and it became as bright as day, but they did not see the light. When they thought I was asleep, the older one touched the younger one and they got up and girded themselves and stretched their hands toward heaven. I could see them but they could not see me and I saw the demons lighting upon the younger one like flies; some were flying while others were lighting upon his eyes and mouth. I saw an angel of the Lord, a flaming sword in his hand, circle around him, chasing away the demons, for they did not dare come near the older one.

[211] " ' "When dawn came they lay down again while I pretended to be asleep and they did the same. The older one said this single sentence to me, 'Do you want to say the twelve psalms together?' and I said yes. The younger one recited nine psalms[43] of six verses each and an alleluia and at each verse a tongue of flame came out of his mouth and ascended to heaven.[44] I said a few verses by heart and as I was leaving I said, 'Pray for me,' but they in silence continued their rites of repentance.[45] I realized that the older one had attained perfection but the Enemy was still fighting with the younger one. Afterwards, when a few days had passed, the older one fell asleep and three days later the younger one did also." ' '

93.1729CD]). Shenoute specifies that supplemental bread may be given to monks, but no more than three loaves (Layton, "Social Structure and Food Consumption," 47 n. 95). Three loaves may have been the maximum ration given to anchorites, and the offering of all three to a guest by monks is a display of great generosity and hospitality. I wish to thank Daniel Caner for this suggestion.

[42]Coptic lacks: when they were settled.

[43]Gk: five, which number Amélineau also gives in his translation, but the text he prints has a Gk theta with a superlinear stroke, "nine."

[44]Coptic lacks: Likewise with the elder, when he opened his mouth to chant it was like a column of fire which came forth and ascended up to heaven. On praying the psalms, see Robert Taft, "Praise in the Desert," *Worship*, 56 (1982): 513–536.

[45]Gk: But they bowed without saying a word.

"Whenever the old men[46] paid a visit to Abba Macarius, he would take them to their cell, saying, 'Come and see the martyrion[47] of the young foreigners.'"

The Story of the Pagan Priest (Macarius 39; Ward, 137)

9   It was said about Abba Macarius the Egyptian that he was going up one time from Scetis to the monastic settlement of Nitria; when he drew near the place he said to his disciple, "Go on ahead a little." When [212] the disciple had gone ahead he met a pagan, a priest of Padalas,[48] *who was running and carrying a great load of firewood.*[49] The brother [that is, Macarius' disciple] called out to the priest, saying, "Hey you, demon, where are you running?" The priest turned around and came up to him and gave him a beating and left him half dead. Then he picked up the wood and took off running again.

When Abba Macarius had gone a little further, he happened upon the priest and said to him, "Well, hello there! You certainly are working hard!"

[46]Gk: fathers.

[47]A martyr's shrine.

[48]I have not been able to identify this deity, which Gk lacks; the word may be corrupted. On non-Christian religion in Egypt at this time, see David Frankfurter, *Religion in Roman Egypt: Assimilation and Resistance* (Princeton: Princeton University Press, 1998).

[49]Instead of "firewood" (*nshe mpikauma*), Greek has "a piece of wood" or stick (*xulon*). David Frankfurter points out, "'Things Unbefitting Christians': Violence and Christianization in Fifth-Century Panopolis," *Journal of Early Christian Studies*, 8:2 (2000): 273–95, that this piece of wood, "as an attribute of the priest and as an incitement to the first monk's rudeness" (285 n. 35), may have held a (pagan) Egyptian sacred image; such images, "many of which were indeed of wood, seem to have borne the brunt of Coptic monks' iconoclastic energy" (283). Shenoute "commonly employed 'piece of wood' as a polemical label for indigenous sacred images" (284). The original context of the wood seems to have been lost in transmission from Greek and the focus shifted in other languages from the wood as idolatrous image, which the monk reacts against and mocks, to its being firewood or a staff which the pagan priest uses as a weapon.

Astonished, the priest stopped and said to him, "What good do you see in me that you honor me by speaking to me?"

The old man said to him, "I saw how hard you were working and you didn't realize that you were working in vain."

The priest said to him, "Your greeting made me think and I realized that you have a great god[50] on your side. But when another monk, a wicked one, met me he cursed me. I beat him within an inch of his life."

The old man realized that the priest was referring to his disciple. Then the priest grabbed his feet and said to him, "I will not let go of you if you do not make me a monk!"

They went up to where the brother lay and carried him to the settlement's church, [213] and when the monks saw the priest they were astonished. They *baptized him and* made him a monk and numerous pagans became Christians on account of him.

Abba Macarius said, "One evil word causes other good words to be bad, just as one good word causes other evil words to become pleasing."

Abba Macarius Sleeps in a Pagan Tomb (Macarius 13; Ward, 130)

10   He also went up one time from Scetis to Terenuthis. He entered a tomb and went to sleep. There were some old bodies[51] of dead pagans there and he took one and put it under his head like a pillow *in order to rest a little.* When the demons saw his courage, *like that of a lion,* they were envious of him and tried to frighten him. They called out a woman's name, saying, "So and so, come with us to the baths." Another demon answered them from below him as though from the dead, "There's a stranger on top of me and I can't come."

---

[50]Gk: God (*tou theou*); the Coptic *ounishti nnouti* would seem to offer an earlier reading, one that a pagan priest might say.

[51]*Sōma*; Gk *skēnōmata*, "corpses," which Ward mistranslates as "coffins" (see Lampe, 1237B-1238A, esp. 2 and 3).

But the old man was not afraid; instead, he decisively knocked on the body, saying, "Get up and go to the darkness, if you are able." [214] When the demons heard this, they cried out in a loud voice, "You have prevailed over us," and they left, ashamed.

Abba Macarius Teaches a Brother to Be Dead to the World
(Macarius 23; Ward, 132)[52]

11   A brother paid a visit to Abba Macarius the Great[53] and said to him, "My father, tell me a word how I may be saved."

The old man said to him, "Go to the tombs, abuse the dead, and throw stones at them."[54]

So the brother went and abused them and came and told the old man. The old man said to him, "Didn't they say anything to you?"

He said, "No."

The old man said to him, "Go tomorrow and praise them, saying, 'You are apostles and saints and righteous people.'"[55]

He returned to the old man and said, "I praised them," and the old man said to him, "Didn't they say anything in reply?"

He said, "No."

The old man said to him, "You saw how you abused them and they did not say anything to you and how you praised them and they said nothing in reply; it's the same with you: if you wish to be saved, go, be dead, take no account of people's scorn or their compliments, like the dead themselves, and you can be saved."

---

[52]This saying occurs in the *Virtues of Saint Macarius 6*.

[53]Gk: Abba Macarius the Egyptian.

[54]For a similar action, see *AP* Anoub 1. Gk locates throwing the stones in the next sentence.

[55]Gk has "You are apostles and saints and righteous people" in the next sentence.

Abba Macarius Welcomes Rebuke (Macarius 31; Ward, 134)

12   *Again* it was said about him that if a brother came to him fearfully as though to a saint and great old man, he would say nothing
to him. [215] But if one of the brothers heaped scorn on him, saying,
"My father, when you were a camel-driver and stole nitre and sold
it, didn't the guards beat you?"[56] If someone said these words to him,
he would speak with them [*sic*] with joy about whatever they [*sic*]
asked him.

*Abba Macarius Helps an Old Woman Find a Deposit (Macarius 7;
Ward, 128–29)*

13   Abba Sisoës said, "When I was in Scetis with *Abba* Macarius, we
went up with him, seven of us, to work the harvest.[57] Listen here: a
widow was gleaning[58] behind us and she would not stop weeping.
So the old man called to the owner of the field and said to him,
'What's the matter with this old woman who weeps all the time?'

"He said to him, 'Her husband received a deposit from someone
and he died suddenly and hadn't told her where he had put it, and
the owner of the deposit wants to seize her and her children as
slaves.'[59]

"The old man said to him, 'Tell her to come to us where we are
resting during the heat.'

"When she came, the old man said to her, 'Why are you weeping
all the time?'

"She said to him, 'My husband received a deposit from someone
and he didn't tell me where he put it.'

[56]For "Macarius the camel-driver," see *Life of Macarius of Scetis* 8.

[57]On monks gleaning, see Syriac *Life of Symeon* 11. I wish to thank Daniel Caner
for this reference.

[58]Ward's "cried out behind us" is a mistake, reading the participle of *kalamoun*
as *kalein*.

[59]The papyri testify to such actions by creditors (*P. Lond.* VI 1915–16).

"The old man said to her, 'Come, show me where you buried[60] him.' He took the brothers with him and left [216] with her and when they came to the place the old man said to her, 'Go home.' While they prayed, the old man called to the dead man, saying, 'So and so, where did you put the other man's deposit?'

"He replied and said, 'It's in my house, beneath the foot of the bed.'

"The old man said to him, 'Now you can rest until the day of resurrection.'

"When the brothers saw this, they fell at his feet in fear. The old man said to them, 'It was not on account of me that this happened, for I am nothing, but it was for the sake of this widow and her orphans that God has done this. This is what is great: that God wants the soul to be without sin.'[61] And they[62] went and told the widow where the deposit was and she took it and gave it to its owner and freed her children. Those[63] who heard about this gave glory to God."

Abba Macarius Teaches about Silence (Macarius 16; Ward, 131)

14 Abba Macarius the Great dismissed the congregation from Scetis and said to the brothers, "Flee, brothers."

An old man said to him, "Where shall we flee beyond this desert?"

He placed his finger on his mouth and said, "This is flight," that is, silence.[64]

---

[60]In Coptic "buried" (*chaf*) and "put" (*chas*) are the same verb, *chō*, with different pronominal suffixes.

[61]Coptic lacks "and grants it all it asks."

[62]Gk: he.

[63]Gk: All.

[64]The end of the sentence, "that is, silence," which Gk lacks, is clearly an explanatory gloss. Gk concludes: and he went into his cell, shut the door, and sat down.

Abba Macarius Teaches Paphnutius How to Be Saved (Macarius 28; Ward, 133)

15   Abba Paphnutius, the disciple of Abba Macarius, said, [217] "I begged the old man, 'My father, tell me a word.'

"He said to me, 'Do not do anything evil and do not judge anyone, and you will be saved.' "

Abba Macarius Tells Moses where to Find Solitude (Macarius 22; Ward, 132)

16   Abba Moses said to Abba Macarius,[65] "I wish to live in solitude, but the brothers won't let me."

Abba Macarius said to him, "I see that you are soft-hearted and are unable to turn away a brother. If you truly wish to live alone, listen to me: go[66] to Petra[67] and you will find solitude."

And he did as Abba Macarius said and found peace.

Anger Is a Passion that Destroys (Macarius 17; Ward, 131)

17   Abba Macarius said, "If you rebuke someone and do it with anger, you have allowed a passion to control you. You have not saved anyone and have destroyed yourself."

[65]Coptic lacks: at Scetis. This could easily have been added to the text as the sayings moved out of Egypt.

[66]Coptic lacks: to the interior desert.

[67]On Petra, see *The Coptic Encyclopedia*, ed. Aziz S. Atiya (New York: Macmillan, 1991), 4.1315. This Petra, Jabal Khashm al-Qu'ud, may have been one of three locales: 20 miles west of the Wadi al-Natrun (Scetis), partially excavated in 1932 by Omar Toussoun, who believed he was working at the site of Kellia; Pherme, mentioned by Palladius (*LH* 20) and Sozomen (*EH* 6.29), an identification accepted by Derwas Chitty; or Calamus, mentioned by John Cassian.

Human Friendships Remove One from God

18 *Again he said, "There is no doubt that whoever seeks human friendships has removed himself from friendship with God, for it is written, 'Woe to you when everyone speaks well of you' " [Lk 6:26].*[68]

Seeking Righteousness over Pleasure

19 *Again he said, "This is what I think: if you act according to human pleasures, they will themselves find fault with you for being without* [218] *fear;*[69] *if they are zealous for righteousness, however, even if they suffer a little, their conscience will not allow them to be blind to God's will."*[70]

Abba Macarius Tells the Monks at Nitria to Weep (Macarius 34; Ward, 136)

20 *I heard*[71] *that* the old men of the monastic settlement *of Nitria* sent once for Abba Macarius the Great in Scetis, beseeching him and saying to him, "So that all the people don't come to you,[72] we pray that you will come to us so we may see you before you go to the Lord."

When he went to the community, all the people congregated around him and the old men begged him, "Speak a word to the brothers," but he wept and said to them, "Let us weep *for ourselves,*

[68]This seems to be a warning against human friendships that come at the expense of friendship with God; in Lk 6:26 Jesus warns his listeners that their ancestors also spoke well of *false* prophets.

[69]Apparently it means being without the fear of God.

[70]"God's will" is literally "what is according to [*kata*] God" and thus parallels its opposite, "according to [*kata*] human pleasures."

[71]Gk narrates this saying in the third person.

[72]Gk: so that all the people are not troubled.

brothers!" and "May our eyes pour tears before we go where our tears will burn our bodies."

They all wept and threw themselves on their faces, saying, "Pray for us, our father!"

"I Have Not Yet Become a Monk but I Have Seen Monks" (Macarius 2; Ward, 125–26)[73]

21   *I heard*[74] *that* Abba Macarius the Egyptian left Scetis one time for the monastic settlement of Nitria for the offering of Abba Pambo and the old men said to him, "Speak a word to the brothers, our father."

But he said, "I have not yet become a monk, but I have seen monks. Once while I was sitting in my cell in Scetis, I thought to myself, 'Go to the desert [219] and learn from what you see there.' This thought remained with me for five years as I said, 'Perhaps it comes from the demons.' The thought persisted, though, so I went into the desert. I found a marshy lake and an island in the middle, and the beasts of the desert came there to drink, and I saw two men in the midst of the animals and they were naked. I trembled all over with fear because I thought they were spirits.

"When they saw that I was shaking with fear, they said to me, 'Do not be afraid. We too are men.'

"I said to them, 'Where are you from, and why did you come to this desert?'

"They said, 'We come from a monastery. We agreed to come here forty years ago. One of us is an Egyptian and the other is a Libyan.' They now questioned me: 'How is the world?' and 'Is the Nile rising on time?' and 'Is the world enjoying prosperity?'

"I said to them, 'By the grace of God and your prayers.'[75] Then I asked them how I could become a monk.

---

[73]Another version of this story appears as *Life of Macarius of Scetis* 28.

[74]Gk narrates this saying in the third person.

[75]Gk: I said to them, "Yes." The Coptic reflects a spirituality that one does not

"They said to me, 'If one does not renounce all worldly things, [220] he can not become a monk.'

"I said to them, 'I am weak; I can not be like you.'

"They said to me, 'If you can not be like us, sit in your cell and weep for your sins.'

"I asked them, 'When winter comes, don't you freeze? And when it gets hot, don't your bodies burn?'

"They said to me, 'God has ordained this for us. We neither freeze in the winter nor burn up in the summer.'

"This is why I told you 'I have not yet become a monk but I have seen monks.' Forgive me, brothers."

Abba Macarius Became a God upon Earth (Macarius 32; Ward, 134)

22 It was said of Abba Macarius the Great that he became a god upon earth, as it is written [Jn 10:34–36].[76] Just as God protects the world, so too did Abba Macarius cover[77] shortcomings: when he saw them it was as though he did not see them and when he heard them it was as though he did not hear them.

usually find in the *Apophthegmata*, but readily occurs in other ancient monastic documents such as the *Historia Monachorum* and Serapion of Thmuis' letter on the death of Antony.

[76]This assertion about Macarius is also found in the *Virtues of Saint Macarius* 1, 32, and 74, and the Coptic *Life of Macarius of Scetis* 34. In the *Virtues*, the narrator says that "the voice of the Lord" had come to Macarius and proclaimed him "a god upon earth." Lucien Regnault, *The Day-to-Day Life of the Desert Fathers in Fourth-Century Egypt* (Petersham, MA: Saint Bede's, 1999), x, has observed that this title was held by pharaohs in ancient Egypt. He also notes that the title is given to the bishop in *Apostolic Constitutions* 11.26; see also Peter Brown, *The Making of Late Antiquity* (Cambridge, MA: Cambridge University Press, 1978), 98–102, and Graham Gould, *The Desert Fathers on Monastic Community* (Oxford: Clarendon, 1993), 124 n. 78.

[77]See also *Virtues* 1, 32, and 74; the *Life of Macarius of Scetis* 34; and *Alphabetical Apophthegmata* Poemen 64. Coptic *hōbs* and Gk *skepazein* mean both "cover" and "protect"; an etymological echo of this may be heard in English in "protect," which derives from Latin *tegere*, to cover. The modern Coptic Liturgy of Saint Basil considers "covering" (*skepazein*) a divine attribute: God "has covered us, helped us, guarded us, accepted us, spared us, supported us, and has brought us [safely] to this hour."

Abba Macarius Teaches about Prayer (Macarius 19; Ward, 131)

23   Some old men[78] asked Abba Macarius, saying, "How should one pray?"

   The old man told them, "It is not necessary to say a lot of words; just stretch your hands up to God and say, 'Lord, as you will and as you desire, lead me.'[79] And if you are afflicted, say, 'Lord, [221] help me!' He knows what is good. He will take pity on us *in accordance with his mercies and his love of humanity.*"

Abba Sisoës Tells about Abba Macarius

24   *Abba Sisoës said about Abba Macarius that a brother came to visit him one time and saw the power of God going with him.*[80] *The old man said to himself, "Oh! How this man's weeping*[81] *over sins compares with the virtues!"*

   Abba Macarius said to the brother, "Believe me, if you knew who is with you, you would not fear anything the world has to offer."

Abba Macarius Shows Humility with Regard to His Power

25   *Abba Macarius and Abba Pambo were walking in the mountains one time. Abba Pambo seized Abba Macarius' hands and kissed them, saying, "Power will come forth from these small hands!"*[82]

---

[78]Gk: Some people (*tines*).

[79]Gk: as you will, and as you know, have mercy.

[80]Power from God and its residing with Macarius is an important concept in the *Virtues of Saint Macarius.*

[81]There is a play on words in Coptic: *pirimi* (the weeping) *nte* (of) *pirōmi* (the man).

[82]The sentence "Power will come forth from these small hands," set in a completely different context, occurs in *AP* Macarius 4 (Ward, 128).

Abba Macarius said to him, "Please be quiet, Pambo, my brother. How your words have become blows that wound me!"[83]

Abba Macarius' Ascetic Practice of Weaving Mats[84]

26 *It was said of Abba Macarius the Great that he was in a monastery one time. If the brothers handed in a mat each day, he would himself* [222] *hand in three every day. When the brothers saw this, they said to the abbot,*[85] *"Unless this foreign brother hands in one mat every day, we will not allow him to live with us."*

When the abbot went to Abba Macarius' cell, wishing to speak with him, he stopped outside the cell. He heard that with every slap of his foot that he made he stood up and prayed and offered three acts of repentance.[86] *The abbot immediately returned and said, "Bring me one of Abba Macarius' mats." When they brought it, he took it and threw it into the bakery oven and after a long time, when they were stoking the oven, he ordered the fire to be put out. He saw that the mat had not burned at all and was lying in the fire, and the abbot said to the brothers, "Manual work without ascetic practice is nothing."*

[83]This saying is of interest because Pambo is usually associated with Nitria, while Macarius was at Scetis, although #21 (=Gk Macarius 2) mentions that Macarius crossed the forty miles of desert to go to Pambo's eucharist up in Nitria.

[84]A longer version of this story seems to be *Life of Macarius of Alexandria* 7 (see the companion volume to this one, *Four Desert Fathers*), where the visit is attributed to the Alexandrian.

[85]*Papa*, a term that also occurs in the *Virtues of Saint Macarius*. Lampe, 1006, s.v. *papas*, translates the word as "papa, father," and says it was used as a title of respect of priests and bishops, and especially of the bishop of Alexandria, but does not cite monastic usage.

[86]Probably prostrations, elsewhere called *metanoias*, literally "repentances." This Egyptian practice appears to have traveled to Syria: John of Ephesus, in "Lives of Thomas and Stephen" [*Lives of the Eastern Saints* 13, *Patrologia Orientalis* 18.204], describes one act of penance this way: "During every [interval], he would make thirty Egyptian metunâyē [= *metanoiai*] which are called prayers, until he accomplished five hundred during the night with the service of matins, and these I myself on many nights secretly counted." I wish to thank Daniel Caner for this reference.

Abba Macarius Teaches Abba Macarius the Alexandrian about Compassion (Macarius 21; Ward, 131–32)

27   It was said of a brother[87] in Scetis that he fell one time due to temptation and that he went to Abba Macarius the Alexandrian and told him about the temptation.[88] After the old man punished him with the bonds of asceticism so he would repent and not open his door for a time, the brother left;[89] *he was troubled, however, because of the temptation and* [223] *was in danger and was not able to carry out the order that Abba Macarius had bound him with. Distressed by battle,[90] he[91] got up and went to where the other Abba Macarius, the* Egyptian, lived.[92] *He told him about the transgression that he had fallen into and about his inability to carry out the order that Abba Macarius had bound him with.*

The old man calmed the brother's spirit and encouraged him in numerous ways, saying, "Go, my child. That which you are able to do, do; gird yourself not to ever commit that sin again." This was his penance.

The brother said to him, "What shall I do? I am troubled on account of the order that Abba Macarius has bound me with."

The old man said to him, "This order does not bind you; rather, it binds Apa [*sic*] Macarius."[93]

When Abba Macarius the Alexandrian heard that the old man had told the brother "This order binds Abba Macarius,"[94] he got up

[87]Gk has two brothers throughout. One wonders if a later editor in Coptic suspected that the transgression of *two* brothers severe enough to warrant excommunication might be sexual and so changed it to one brother.

[88]As priest of Kellia, Macarius of Alexandria would have had the right to impose a penance. The story raises the question why the Alexandrian would have submitted himself to the authority of the Egyptian and substantiates the Alexandrian's harsh asceticism. See Evagrius *Praktikos* 94; Antoine Guillaumont, "Le problème des deux Macaires"; Gabriel Bunge, "Évagre le Pontique et les deux Macaires."

[89]Gk simply states that Abba Macarius excommunicated (*echorisen*) them.

[90]Thus Codex 64; Codex 59 specifies "two battles" or "wars" (*-polemos*).

[91]Gk: some brothers.

[92]Gk: Some brothers came and told Abba Macarius the Great of Egypt about it.

[93]Gk: It is not the brothers who are excommunicated; it is Macarius (for he loved him).

[94]Gk: Hearing that he had been excommunicated by the old man.

and fled into the marsh; *he resolved to remain there, without coming into contact with anyone, until he completed the sentence that he had bound on* [224] *the brother.*

He remained in the marsh many days until his body was swollen with mosquito bites. *Abba Macarius the Egyptian heard that the old man had fled to the marsh on account of what he had said.* The other Macarius got up and went to the marsh and looked for Abba Macarius the Alexandrian until he found him. When he saw him, he said to him, "Venerable sir, I said what I did in order to encourage that brother, and you, when you heard,[95] like a good virgin fled into the interior bedchamber. *Get up, then, my father, return to your cell.*"[96]

Abba Macarius the Alexandrian said, "Forgive me according to the terms of what you told the brother, because what you said applies to me. Unless I complete the sentence that I bound on the brother, I will not leave."[97]

When Abba Macarius the Egyptian saw that he was firm in his decision to patiently endure his sentence,[98] *he encouraged him like this: "No; get up. Come with me and I will show you what you need to do."*

So persuaded, Abba Macarius the Alexandrian got up and went with him. Abba Macarius the Egyptian spoke with him on familiar terms. He said to him, "Go, spend this year[99] eating once a week."

This was not an order that he bound him with since before Abba Macarius the Egyptian had even spoken it, [225] it was already the ascetic practice of Abba Macarius the Alexandrian to eat once a week.

---

[95]Gk: So you have excommunicated some brothers; and yet they live apart in the village. I myself have excommunicated you and . . .

[96]Gk: I have summoned the two brothers, and have learnt from them what happened, and I have told them nothing has happened. Examine yourself, then, my brother, and see if you have not been the sport of demons.

[97]In Gk this paragraph is: Then the other asked him, "Please give me a penance."

[98]Gk: Faced with his humility.

[99]Gk: three weeks.

Abba Macarius Warns against Gluttony

28 Abba Macarius said, *"Whoever fills himself with bread and water gives the key to his house to robbers at the same time.*[100]

Abba Macarius Never Tires of Beseeching Christ

29 *... and afterwards when he visited him [Abba Macarius, presumably], he heard him weeping and crying out, "Jesus, Jesus, if my cries do not ring in your ears when I call out day and night to you in heaven to have mercy on me and to pity me on account of my sins, I will still not grow tired of imploring you."*[101]

Abba Macarius' Conversation with a Skull (Macarius 38; Ward, 136–37)

30 *It was said*[102] *about* Abba Macarius the Great that while walking in the mountain[103] one time he saw the head of a dead man lying upon the mountain. He moved the head,[104] and it spoke to him. The old man said to it, "Who are you *who speak to me like this?*"

[100]Amélineau joins this saying with the next (with ellipses). Clearly something has dropped out of the text: the next portion reads like a separate saying, and I have numbered it as such. Saying 28 exists independently in the *Virtues of Saint Macarius* 45, which shows that 28 and 29 are separate sayings, as Regnault, 193, realizes.

[101]This may be a reference to the Jesus Prayer; see *Virtues* #13, 34, 35, 41, 42, and 44. For a discussion, see Antoine Guillaumont, "The Jesus Prayer Among the Monks of Egypt," *Eastern Churches Review*, 6 (1974): 66–71. Another valuable discussion is Kallistos Ware, "The Origins of the Jesus Prayer: Diadochus, Gaza, Sinai," in Cheslyn Jones, Geoffrey Wainwright, Edward Yarnold, eds., *The Study of Spirituality* (New York: Oxford University Press, 1986), 175–184. On the related issue of unceasing prayer, see Lucien Regnault, "La prière continuelle 'monologistos' dans la littérature apophtegmatique," *Irénikon*, 47 (1974): 467–93, reprinted in *Les Pères du désert à travers leur Apophtegmes* (Solesmes, 1987), 113–39. See also Gabriel Bunge, " 'Priez sans cesse': aux origines de la prière hésychaste," *Studia Monastica*, 30 (1988): 7–16.

[102]Gk has Macarius narrating the story.

[103]Gk: desert.

[104]Coptic lacks: with my stick.

The skull said to him, "I was a pagan[105] during the time of the pagans.[106] *I have been allowed to speak with you."*

The old man said to him, "And I, who am I?"

The skull said to him, "You are *Abba* Macarius the Spiritbearer."[107]

The old man said to him, "Are you at peace, or do you suffer?"

The skull [226] *said to him, "I am being punished."*

The old man said to him, "What sort of punishment is it?"

The skull said to him, "Just as the sky is high over the earth, so too is there a river of fire boiling over our heads and underneath us, lapping over our feet. We stand in the middle, unable to look at one another because our backs are joined to each other. But at the moment when someone[108] offers a great supplication for us, *we gain a little peace."*

The old man said to him, "What is this peace?"

The skull said to him, "For the blink of an eye we see each other's faces."

When the old man heard this, he wept and cried out, "*If this is the peace that punishment brings,*[109] then woe to the woman who lies with a man in order to bear a child![110] *It would be better if children were never brought into the world!"* The old man said to him, "Are there worse punishments than yours?"

The skull said to him, "*Yes, for* below us is punishment whose fire—whose terrible fire—is even darker and more pitiless."

The old man said to him, "Are there people in this fire?"

The skull said to him, "Yes, there are some there." The skull continued speaking, "As for us, since [227] we did not know God, we

---

[105]Gk: high priest.

[106]Coptic lacks: who dwelt in this place.

[107]Coptic lacks: Whenever you take pity on those who are in torments, and pray for them, they feel a little respite. On Macarius as "Spiritbearer," see *Virtues of Saint Macarius* 83.

[108]In Gk the skull tells Macarius that *his* prayers alleviate the suffering.

[109]This first part of the sentence is added by one Gk MS.

[110]The Gk is more specific: "Alas the day when that man was born!" (Ward, 137).

were not cast into this punishment below, but those who know God and reject him have been cast below us."[111]

Abba Macarius and the Dead Man in the Tomb

31   It was said about Abba Macarius the Great that he spent three years living in a tomb in which there was a dead man. After the three years, when Abba Macarius wanted to leave the place, the dead man stood in front of the door and said, "I will not let you leave, my father!"

The old man said, "Why?"

The dead man said to him, "Before you entered this tomb, I was consigned to great suffering and affliction, but when you came and lived here I found peace because of you. I am afraid, therefore, that if I allow you to leave, my suffering and affliction will come back again."

As the dead man stood in front of the door to the tomb, there came a voice, "Let the man of God leave, for if some small acts of righteousness had not been found in you so that because of them pity might be taken on you, God would not have sent his servant to spend these three years in this tomb in order that, because of him, pity might be taken on you."

Abba Macarius Defeats the Demon of Profit

32   It was said about Abba Macarius that he happened to be in the wadi gathering palm branches, and when he had finished collecting them [228] and they had all been gathered so he could tie them together, a demon came upon him in the form of a monk who seemed to be harsh and angry. He said to him, "Macarius, do not tie the palm leaves together until you give me my share."

The old man said to him, "Come, take what you want."

[111]Coptic lacks "Then, picking up the skull, the old man buried it."

The demon said to him, "Divide them. Give me part and take part for yourself too."

The old man divided them and made one part larger than the other and said to the demon, "Take whichever of these two you want."

The demon said to him, "No, you did all the work. You go first; take whichever pile you want."

The old man took the smaller portion and immediately the demon cried out, "You are powerful, Macarius! I have defeated numbers of people, but you have defeated me!"[112]

The old man said to him, "Who are you, then?" and the demon said to him, "I am the demon of profit."

And when the old man said a prayer, the demon disappeared.

Abba Macarius and the Two Devout Laywomen

33   Again it was said about Abba Macarius that one time when he was praying in his cell a voice came to him, saying, "Macarius, you have not yet reached [229] the level of two women who live in such-and-such a village."[113]

When the old man got up early in the morning, he took his palm-tree staff and set out on his journey. When he reached the village, an angel walked with him, guiding him to the house. When he knocked at the door, the women opened it to him. When they realized it was Abba Macarius, they did obeisance to him on the ground and received him with joy. The old man said to them, "On account of you I have patiently endured the hardships of this journey through the desert and have come here. Tell me, therefore, what is your way of life?"

They, however, wanting to conceal their way of life, said to him, "Why do you inquire about the way of life of those who are defiled?"

After the old man had asked their forgiveness, he said to them, "Do not hide anything from me, for it is God who has sent me."

[112]See *Life of Antony* 6.1.
[113]A reference to this may be found in the *Life of Macarius of Scetis* 33.

*They became fearful and revealed everything to him, saying, "For-
give us, our father. The two of us are strangers to each other according
to the world, but by mutual agreement, we have been made two ‹sisters›*[114] *according to the flesh. Look, it has been fifteen years today that
we have lived in this house and we do not recall that we have ever quar-
reled with one another or that one of us has ever said an idle word to
her companion. On the contrary, we are always at peace [230] and of
one mind. We agreed to leave our husbands and to exchange married
life for the life of virginity. But when we implored our husbands over
and over concerning what we wanted, they did not agree to let us go.
When we could not accomplish our goal, we drew up a covenant
between ourselves and God that to the day of our death our mouths
would not speak a worldly utterance but that we would direct our
thoughts to God and his saints at all times and would devote ourselves
unceasingly to prayers and fastings and acts of charity."*

*When Abba Macarius heard these things, he said, "Truly, it is not
the name of 'monk' or 'layperson' or 'virgin' or 'wife and husband' but
an upright disposition that God seeks, and he gives his Holy Spirit to
all of these people."*

*And after the old man had profited from meeting the two women,
he returned to his cell, clapping his hands and saying, "I have not been
at peace with my brothers like these lay women have with one another."*

*Abba Macarius Gives Instruction to Theopemptus (Macarius 3;
Ward, 126–27)*

34 *It was said about* Abba Macarius the Great *that* when he lived in
the interior desert he lived alone there as an anchorite. [231] Further
to the interior[115] was another desert where some other brothers lived.
The old man was watching the road one time when he saw Satan

---

[114]Amélineau translates "two sisters," but the text he prints has *-son*, "brothers,"
instead of *sōni*, "sisters."
[115]Thus Codex 64; Codex 59 has "to the north," but see below. Gk: lower down.

approaching, dressed like a traveler.[116] He looked like he was wearing a linen tunic full of holes and from each hole there hung a pot.

Abba Macarius[117] said to him, "*Old man, where are you going?*" and he said, "I'm on my way to stir up the brothers' thoughts."

Abba Macarius said to him, "What are you going to do with those pots?" and he said to him, "I'm taking various kinds of food for the brothers to taste."

Abba Macarius said to him, "All of these?"

The Devil answered and said to the old man,[118] "If this one does not please one of the brothers, I offer him another; if that one does not please him, I offer him yet another. Certainly one of them has to please him!" After saying these things, he left.

The old man sat down and watched the road until the Devil returned. When the old man saw him, he said to him, "Hello. How are you?"

The Devil said to him, "Why do you care how I am?" and Abba Macarius said to him, "What do you mean?"

The Devil said to him, "The brothers were all rude to me [232] and not one of them welcomed me."

Abba Macarius replied and said, "You didn't make a single friend there?" and the Devil replied and said, "I did make one friend there and he obeys me. When he sees me, he comes running like the wind."[119]

The old man said to him, "And what is his name?" and he said to Abba Macarius, "His name is Theopemptus." When he had said these things, he left.

Abba Macarius got up and went into the desert interior to his own[120] and when the brothers heard about it they brought palm

[116]Gk: like a person, and he passed by him.
[117]Gk: The old man
[118]Gk: He said, "Yes."
[119]Codex 64 reads *anebi*, which Amélineau translates "un petit animal," but Codex 59 has *anemi*, which must be an attempted transliteration of Greek *anemos* and agrees with the Greek text: he changes like the wind.
[120]Gk: the desert below his own.

branches and came out to greet him [Jn 12:12–13].[121] *What is more,*
each one got himself ready thinking that Abba Macarius would rest
himself with him in his home. But the old man asked, "Where does
the brother called 'Theopemptus' live in this settlement?" and when
he found out, he went to his cell.

Theopemptus received him *eagerly and* with joy. The old man
began to discuss the matter with him and said to him, "Tell me about
your thoughts, my child,"[122] and he said to Abba Macarius, "Pray for
me and I will prosper."

The old man said to him, "Don't your thoughts fight against
you?" and he said to Abba Macarius, "Up to now I have prospered,"
for he was ashamed to tell the truth.

The old man said to him, "To this day I have practiced asceticism
these many years and [233] every one honors me. I am an old man
and the spirit of fornication still troubles me."[123]

Theopemptus replied and said to him, "Believe me, my father, I
too have this trouble."

The old man, giving himself permission to speak, spoke of other
thoughts that fought against him until Theopemptus confessed.
Then the old man said to him, "How do you fast?" and he said to
him, "Until the ninth hour."[124]

The old man said to him, "Fast until evening[125] *and keep your
ascetic practices* and recite by heart the Gospel[s] and the rest of the
Scriptures and if a thought[126] comes to you do not look down to it
but look upwards at all times and God will help you."

When the old man had finished instructing the brother, he left
for his own desert. As the old man was watching the road, he saw that
same demon and said to him, "Where are you going?"

---

[121]Apparently a common practice.

[122]Gk: How are you getting on, brother?

[123]On the spirit of fornication, see *Life of Antony* 6.2.

[124]The ninth hour, or about three p.m., was the time the monks usually ate their
daily meal.

[125]Gk: Practice fasting a little later.

[126]Gk: a foreign thought.

He said to Abba Macarius, "I want to stir up the brothers' thoughts." When he returned, therefore, the saint said to him, "How did it go with the brothers?" and he said to him, "Badly."

The old man said to him, "Why?" and he said to Abba Macarius, "They were all rude to me, and the worst one was that one who was my friend and who used to obey me. [234] I don't know why he changed. Not only does he no longer obey me, but he has become the rudest of them all! I've sworn not to set foot there again, at least not for a while."

When he had said these things, he departed and left the old man and the saint went inside his cell.

Glory to the Father and to the Son and to the Holy Spirit for ever and ever. Amen.

Lord, have mercy on your servant Matoi.[127]

---

[127]Matoi is presumably either the scribe or translator.

CHAPTER TWO

The Virtues of Saint Macarius of Egypt

SYNOPTIC TABLE

Comparing the Virtues of Macarius *with the Greek and Coptic* Alphabetical Apophthegmata *and the Greek Systematic Apophthegmata*[1]

Virtues	Greek Alph.	Greek Sys.	Coptic Alph.
1. A Cherub Calls	(32)		(22)[2]
2. Defeating the Devil	11	XV.40	6
3. Healing a Procurator's Daughter			7[3]
4. Antony, Macarius' Teacher			
5. The Good God, Holy Power, and Paraclete[4]			
6. Telling a Brother to Imitate the Dead	23		11
7. Teaching a Brother about Obedience			
8. Giving Counsel to Abba Poemen			
9. Teaching about Judgment and Mercy			
10. Teaching about Trust in God			
11. Teaching about the Passions			
12. Teaching about Christ's Sweetness			
13. Speaking to Abba Poemen			
14. Healing an Antelope's Young			
15. Speaking about Scetis' Devastation	5	XVIII.16	

---

[1]Many of the cross-references in this table are from Lucien Regnault, *Les Sentences des Pères du désert: Troisieme recueil et tables* (Solesmes, 1976), 151–191.

[2]Part of *AP* Macarius the Great 32 (Coptic 22) is embedded in #1, #32 and #74.

[3]This story can also be found in the *Sayings of Saint Macarius* 7 (Am, 207), and *Life of Saint Macarius of Scetis* 32 (Am, 101–5).

[4]This "saying" is also known as the *Letter of Macarius* (PG 34.407–10) or *Ad filios Dei*; see #5 below and the first note there.

16. Speaking about Scetis' Renewal
17. Telling Evagrius about Free Will
18. Listing the Monastic Virtues   (JK 34)[5]   I.13, I.16[6]
19. Concerning Giving Birth in the Spirit
20. Talking about the Mustard Seed
21. Explaining the Parable Further
22a-c. Three Sayings
23. Teaching about Repentance
24. Further Teaching about Repentance
25. Teaching about Pity and Compassion
26. Teaching about Mercy
27. Teaching about the Soul
28. Further Teaching about the Soul
29. Teaching about Constancy in God
30. Teaching about Fornication and Avarice
31. Receiving Power from Christ
32. Shenoute Marvels at the Monks' Works   (32)   (22)
33. Explaining a Saying by Sisoës[7]
34. Teaching about the Name of Christ
35. Explaining the Above Saying
36. Explaining the Meaning of the Wolf
37. Advising Two Brothers
38. Christ the Compassionate Potter
39. Speaking about Himself
40. Interpreting a Brother's Saying
41. Teaching about Relying upon the Name of Christ
42. Teaching about Calling upon the Name of Christ
43. Telling a Parable about Compassion
44. Recounting a Visit to an Old Man
45. Warning against Gluttony   28
46. Recognizing a Brother's Humility
47. Teaching about What it Takes to Live   20
48. Teaching about Desiring Salvation
49. Teaching about Vigilance
50a. Concerning Nighttime Responsibilities

[5]The Alphabetical Collection attributes this saying to John the Little (John Kolobos); see n. 6 below.
[6]The Greek Systematic Collection attributes a version of this saying to John the Little in I.13 and to Macarius in I.16.
[7]See *AP* Poemen 88.

[8]See *Homily* 33.1 by Pseudo-Macarius and the note at #59 below.

[9]This saying appears to be part of *Ad filios Dei*; see the notes at #5 above and below.

[10]See Nilus *Letters* 3.322 (PG 79.537D–540A).

[11]See Evagrius *Praktikos* 94, and *Life of Macarius of Alexandria* 12 (in the companion volume to this one, *Four Desert Fathers*).

THE VIRTUES OF SAINT MACARIUS[12]

From the Virtues of Our Righteous Father Abba Macarius the Great[13]

A Cherub Calls Abba Macarius to Scetis

1   [118] It was said concerning Abba Macarius that when he had increased in virtue and had come to personify it, giving thanks with great patience, the Lord of Glory sent a cherub:[14] he led him into this mountain and when he had set his seal on Abba Macarius by placing his hands on his breast as though taking its measure, Abba Macarius said to him, "What is this?"

The cherub said to him, "I have weighed your heart."[15]

Abba Macarius said to him, "What do you mean?"

The cherub said to him, "They will name this mountain after your heart; Christ has given it to you as an inheritance. But he will seek its fruits from you."

---

[12]Translated from the text edited by Amélineau, *Histoire*, 118–202, from Cod. Vat. LXIV, fol. 57–112, with corrections made by comparing Amélineau's text with a microfiche of the MS.; for these corrections, see Tim Vivian, "The *Virtues of Saint Macarius*, The Manuscript, and Amélineau's Text," *Coptica*, 1 (2002): 69–76. Paragraphing generally follows that of Amélineau, while paragraph titles and numbers are those of the translator. Page numbers in brackets indicate the pagination of Amélineau's text. There is a French translation of the *Virtues* by Lucien Regnault, "reviewed and corrected by Antoine Guillaumont," in Regnault, *Les Sentences des Pères*, 151–191. Regnault notes that Amélineau's version is error prone.

[13]At the top it reads: "The second Sunday of Lent to the forty-sixth chapter of the book: read."

[14]Text: a cherubim. Both in the *Virtues* and in the *Life of Macarius of Scetis*, Coptic uses plural "cherubim" for the singular. This cherub figures prominently in the *Life* and appears in the iconography of Macarius at the Monastery of Saint Antony; see Elizabeth S. Bolman, ed., *Monastic Visions: The Wall Paintings at the Monastery of St. Antony at the Red Sea* (New Haven: Yale University Press: 2002).

[15]In Coptic, "heart" is *hēt* and "breast" is *meste nhēt*; "measure" or "weigh" is *shi* and "Scetis," the monastic community that Macarius founded, is *shi hēt*. See *Life of John the Little* 16; Maged S. Mikhail and Tim Vivian, trans., "Life of Saint John the Little," 28.

Abba Macarius said to him, [119] "What are these fruits?"

The cherub said to him, "They are spiritual fruits, which are the commandments and virtues, and Christ our God will make you god[16] over this land on which will live a multitude of people. Those who hear and keep and observe your commandments will be a wreath and royal diadem on your head in the presence of Christ the King."

After the cherub had said these things to him, he crucified him[17] on the land and said to him, "You will be crucified with Christ and you will join him on the cross with the virtues adorning you with their perfume, and your ascetic practices will spread[18] to the four corners of the earth and will raise up a multitude sunk in the mire of sin and they will become warriors and soldiers in Christ's army."[19]

Abba Macarius ‹transfixed›[20] his body and perfectly and zealously accomplished everything that the cherub told him.

[16]Although Am translates "le père," the text as he has it, confirmed by the microfiche, reads "god." His translation suggests a reading of *naaik niōt* ("will make you father") instead of *naaik nnouti* (will make you [a] god). But *AP* Macarius the Great 32 (= Coptic 22) declares that "It was said of Abba Macarius the Great that he became a god upon earth, as it is written," and *Virtues* 32 affirms that "the voice of the Lord had come" to Macarius, "saying, 'You have become a god upon the earth.'" In #4 Macarius "esteemed" Antony "as a god"; thus the "divine" patrimony of early monasticism was, according to the tradition itself, passed on from Antony to Macarius.

[17]This is literally what *afashf* means. It is possible that the verb is being used reflexively here: "he [Macarius] crucified [that is, prostrated?] himself," but the subjects of the sentence seem to all be the cherub.

[18]"Spread" translates *-ishi*, from the same root as "crucified," *ash=*; see Crum, 89A (f). The Coptic may also be playing here on *shi*, "weigh, measure," and *ishi*, "crucify, hang."

[19]"Army" translates *-noumeron*, which represents, via Greek, Latin *numerum*. *Numerus* was the generic name for any military unit but was used more specifically of units formed in non-Roman areas such as Egypt.

[20]Am prints *ashi* and translates it "crucifiait" (see above), but the MS. clearly reads *ōfi*, "press," perhaps a mistake for *ōft*, "nail, fix" (see Crum 535B-536A).

Abba Macarius Defeats the Devil with Humility (AP Macarius 11; Coptic 6)

2   When Abba Macarius was passing one time through the wadi to his cell, carrying some palm branches, the Devil met him on the path with a scythe. He tried to strike Abba Macarius but was unable to, and said to him, "You are powerful, Macarius! I can't do anything against you! Look—what you can do, I can do too: you [120] fast and I don't eat anything at all; you keep vigil, and I don't sleep at all. There is only one thing at which you're better than me."

Abba Macarius said to him, "What is that?"

The Devil said to him, "It's your humility. On account of your humility, there is nothing I can do to you."

And when the saint stretched out his hands, the demon disappeared and Abba Macarius continued on his way, giving glory to God.

Abba Macarius Heals a Procurator's Daughter (Coptic Sayings 7, Life of Macarius of Scetis 32)

3   It was said concerning Abba Macarius that Agathonicus, the procurator of Antioch,[21] heard about him, that he had great powers and gifts of healing through our Lord Jesus Christ. He sent him his daughter, who had an unclean spirit, so Abba Macarius might pray over her. By the grace[22] of God that was in him, when he prayed over her she was immediately healed and he sent her in peace to her parents. When her father and mother saw the healing that the Lord had brought about in their daughter through the prayers and intercessions of Saint Abba Macarius, they gave thanks, giving glory to our Savior Jesus Christ.

[21]Procurators were agents of the emperor in the civil administration and were posted to minor provinces such as Judea.
[22]Both "grace" and "gifts" translate Coptic *hmot*.

Antony the Teacher of Abba Macarius[23]

4   Abba Macarius said, "I was passing through the desert one time when the Devil met me; his face was ugly and [121] very fearful, and he said to me, "You are powerful, Macarius! Your fame resounds in the east and in the west, like that of Antony the Great, the leader of solitary monks,[24] and you emulate him, as Elisha emulated Elijah [1 Kings 19:19–21], for Antony himself was your teacher because it was he who clothed you in the monastic habit.[25] Indeed, you have fought me with your humility because you received counsel from Antony in humility and esteemed him as a god through the love engendered by your authentic humility. When I fought you with my weapons, the passions, you would always say right away from the depths of your heart with a firm faith, 'Behold, my doctor and my physician upon the mountain and the ‹river›.'[26]

"I said to him in response, 'I am truly blessed[27] because the Lord Jesus, mindful of you, has strengthened my heart and faith in my teacher. The medicines of my lord and father Abba Antony are not fleshly; no, the power of the Paraclete is at work in his prayers. Spiritual medicines are acceptable to God like incense.'

"When the Devil heard these things, he became like smoke and disappeared and I continued walking, giving glory to our Lord Jesus Christ."

---

[23]On Antony and Macarius, see *AP* Macarius 4, and 26; their relationship (with Macarius as a disciple of Antony) is an important theme in the *Life of Macarius of Scetis* 17 and 19.

[24]*-monachos napotaktikos*. On the *apotaktikoi*, see E. A. Judge, "The Earliest Use of Monachos for 'Monk' (P. Coll. Youtie 77) and the Origins of Monasticism," *Jahrbuch für Antike und Christentum*, 10 (1977): 72–89, and James E. Goehring, "Through a Glass Darkly: Images of the *Apotaktikoi* in Early Egyptian Monasticism," in his *Ascetics, Society, and the Desert*, 53–72.

[25]On his being clothed in the habit by Antony, see *Life of Macarius of Scetis* 19 and the Introduction to this volume.

[26]Text: *niphakhri*, "drugs, medicines," probably picked up from the next paragraph, is clearly a mistake for *phiaro*, "river," the reading Am adopts without a note. The "mountain" would represent the monastic community, as it often does in early monastic literature, and the "river" probably indicates the Nile.

[27]*-makarios*.

The Good God, the Holy Power, and the Paraclete[28]

5   (7.) [122] Abba Macarius said: "The wiles of the Enemy are those called 'night' and 'darkness,' as Paul said, 'We do not belong to night, nor do we belong to darkness, but we belong to the day' [1 Th 5:5–8], for indeed the Son of God is the day and the Devil is the night.

(8.) "But if the heart passes by these wars, once again they besiege the combatant out of ill-will and then they begin to wage war on him with fornication and taking pleasure with children. On account of these wars, therefore, the heart is enfeebled so that it is impossible for the person to safeguard his purity as they make him aware of the seconds and minutes and the hardships of leading a life of virtue and how hard life is. As a result, great suffering and weariness come over the body.

(9.) "But if the heart grows weary in these matters and becomes enfeebled on account of the sufferings caused by these wars, if the person drives evil away from his heart and cries out to God, groaning in his soul and suffering, then the good God who has compassion for his creature sends a holy power that takes possession of the heart and gives him weeping [123] and rejoicing and relief. As a result, he becomes stronger than the enmity opposing him[29] and his enemies are unable to prevail[30] against him because they are afraid of the power that has come upon him. As the apostle Paul proclaims, 'Strive so that you may receive power' [Acts 1:8 and Lk 13:24]. For this

[28]The paragraphing in parentheses refers to the Greek text of *Ad filios Dei*, a large portion of which survives here in Coptic; see Werner Strothmann, ed., *Die syrische Überlieferung der Schriften des Makarios* (2 vols.; Wiesbaden: Harrossowitz, 1981) and, for an English translation, Tim Vivian, "The Good God, the Holy Power, and the Paraclete: 'To the Sons of God' (*Ad filios Dei*) by Saint Macarius the Great," *Anglican Theological Review*, 30.3 (1998): 338–65, repr. in Vivian, *Words to Live By: Journeys in Ancient and Modern Monasticism* (forthcoming).

[29]Literally: "his enmity." The Coptic often changes Gk "enemy" to "enmity." See Antony *Letter* 1.24 (S. Rubenson, *The Letters of St. Antony: Monasticism and the Making of a Saint* [Minneapolis: Fortress, 1995], 198) where "enmity" is the primary reading with "the enemy" as a variant.

[30]Both "prevail" and "strong" render Coptic *jemjom*, related to "power."

is the power that Peter spoke about when he said, 'There is an inheritance that is imperishable and incorruptible that is watching over you, who are being protected by the power of God through faith' [1 Pet 1:4].

(10.) "When the good God sees that the heart is strong against enmity, then he begins to withdraw the power from him. Seeing his free intention,[31] and making use of fear, [God] suddenly allows enmity into him in order to wage war against him with defilements and with the pleasure that comes from seeing and spiritual vanity and haughtiness. The person is like a rudderless ship drifting here and there.

(11.) "When the heart grows very weary on account of enmity, then God, who is good and has compassion for his creature, once again sends to him the holy power and it strengthens his soul and heart and body and all his other members beneath the yoke of the Paraclete, as our Savior Jesus Christ says: "Take my yoke upon you and learn from me, for I am [124] gentle and humble of heart"[Mt 11:29].

(12.) "Then the good God begins to open 'the eyes of the heart' [Eph 1:18] in order [for the person] to acknowledge and honor God with humility and contriteness of heart, as David says: 'A sacrifice to God is a contrite and humble heart' [Ps 51:17].[32] For from the sufferings caused by the wars, humility and contrition take root in the heart.

(13.) "Then the power reveals heavenly things to the mind and heart and [reveals] the songs and glory that will come to those who persevere, [and the power also reveals] that if the person endures numerous sufferings, these are insignificant compared with the honor that God will give to him, as the apostle once again says: 'The sufferings of the present time are not worth comparing to the glory that will be revealed to us' [Rom 8:18]. Then they begin to reveal the

---

[31]Coptic *prohairesis* = Gk *proairesis*.

[32]Ps 50:19 (LXX). "Humble" (*tetapeinōmenēn*) is taken from the second part of v. 19, not quoted here.

punishments before the heart and those who are being punished and many other things, all of which I am not able to declare.

(14.) "And the Paraclete establishes boundaries for the heart, that is, those things that make the soul and the other members pure,[33] and [establishes] great humility and watchfulness and an understanding of watchfulness, and the placing of oneself beneath all of creation, and [the ability] not to be concerned about the evil deeds of any person, and keeping the eyes pure,[34] and guarding [125] the tongue [Jas 3:5, 3:8], and keeping the feet pure,[35] and working righteousness with the hands,[36] and worshiping with prayers, and mortification of the body, and the ability to keep vigil for God. These things are determined for him in moderation and with consideration, not to cause confusion but to bring about what is godly and proper.

(15.) "But if the understanding denigrates the commandments of the Spirit, then the power withdraws and wars break out in the heart, and disturbances, and the passions of the body disturb him on account of the movements and attacks of the enemies.

(16.) "But if the heart turns about and keeps the commandments of the Spirit, it receives protection. Then the person knows that abiding with God is his rest, as David says: 'Lord, because I have cried out to you, I have found the rest that I desired' [Ps 30:2].

(17.) "I am saying that unless a person possesses great humility in his heart and body, and debases himself in all things, and has a great ability to accept contempt, and suffers violence in all things, and keeps his death before him day after day, and renounces material things, and renounces the things of the flesh, he cannot keep the commandments of the Holy Spirit."

[33]Literally: "the purities of the soul and the other members."
[34]Literally: "purity of the eyes."
[35]Literally: "purity of the feet."
[36]Literally: "justice/righteousness of the hands."

Abba Macarius Tells a Brother to Imitate the Dead (AP Macarius 23; Coptic 11)

6   [126] A brother paid a visit to Abba Macarius and said to him, "Tell me a word: How can I be saved?"

The old man said to him, "Go to the tombs. Curse the dead. Throw rocks at them."[37]

The brother left. He cursed the dead and threw rocks at them, and when he returned to the old man, the old man said to him. "They didn't say anything to you, did they?"

The brother said to him, "No, my father."

The old man said to him, "Go tomorrow and glorify them, saying, 'You are apostles, you are saints and righteous.' "

He returned to the old man and said to him, "I glorified them."

The old man said to him, "They didn't say anything to you, did they?"

He said, "No."

The old man said to him, "You have seen how you cursed them and they did not say anything to you, and how you glorified them and they did not respond at all. It should be the same with you, too: if you wish to be saved, go, be dead, having no regard for people's contempt nor their honors, like the dead, and you can be saved."

Abba Macarius Teaches a Brother about Obedience

7   A brother asked Abba Macarius, "Tell me what it is to live in obedience, my father."

Abba Macarius said to him, "It is like rock: if you use the rock to crush the wheat and extract all the filth from it, [127] the wheat becomes pure bread. It is the same with you, my child: the rock is your father; you are the wheat. If you obey your father, he will intercede

---

[37]For a similar action, see *AP* Anoub 1.

with the Lord on your behalf. He[38] will extract all the filth of Satan from you and, instead of pure bread, you too will be a godly son."

Abba Macarius Gives Counsel to Abba Poemen[39]

8   Abba Poemen said, "When I went to visit Abba Macarius, I said to him, 'My father, how do you want me to live with the brothers? If I speak the word to them, they do not listen.'

"He said to me, 'Perhaps they do not listen to you because they are wearing someone else's bridle.'

"I said to him, 'What bridle?'

"Abba Macarius said to me, 'Perhaps they are getting counsel from someone else, for it is written, "The threefold cord is not soon broken" [Eccl 4:12], that is, if you find the brothers perfect in faith and love and humble obedience toward their fathers, they will not break because their hearts are firmly established. Know this: if a faithful man obtains a faithful woman and if the two of them preserve the purity of marriage, they are at peace with one another and are very content, so that their neighbors and friends [128] envy the understanding they have. But if on the other hand the Wicked One is jealous of them, if the husband and wife let their eyes wander out the window of their house and if the husband casts his eye on the beauty of a young woman, or if the wife does likewise: if the husband or wife is leavened by someone outside the marriage, there is no peace between them because they are separated from each other. It is the same with the brothers: if they abandon the counsel of their fathers and take counsel from others, the counsel of their fathers is not sweet to them and they despise it; they murmur both to themselves and to one another until they are separated from God.' "

[38] Ambiguous in Coptic too.

[39] Poemen is one of the most important of the early monks, has the most sayings in the *Apophthegmata*, and seems to have been involved in the editing of that collection.

When Abba Poemen heard these things from Abba Macarius, he marveled at his discernment and understanding.[40] Apa Poemen said to him, "Truly, this is what it is like, my father."[41] Afterwards, he prayed and left, receiving profit, glorifying our Lord Jesus Christ and his servant Abba Macarius.

Abba Macarius Teaches about Judgment and God's Mercy

9   Abba Macarius said, "If you look into a mirror to observe yourself, it will inform you of your beauty [129] or of your ugliness. You cannot hide anything from it nor will it lie to you in any way; no, it produces a lifelike image and reflects back your own image[42] and reproduces all your features and characteristics: if you smile, you see what sort of a smile it is; it will show you that your black hair is black and your gray hair is ‹gray›[43] and it will reveal you to yourself and show you what you really look like.

"It will be the same at the place of judgment, from which one can not flee. There it is not a mirror made by human hands but deeds laid bare that show your likeness and reveal your sins like a noose around your neck.[44] You can not flee from them; no, they stand rebuking you without need of a witness. You are like a ladder[45] in their midst: you are wretched, and words will not help you. The mirror of sins will teach you all of them and they are engraved in your

---

[40]The text switches from first person to third, a fairly common occurrence in Coptic texts.

[41]The text uses "Apa" instead of "Abba" here.

[42]-zōgraphein and -antigraphein.

[43]Text: -ouash, which is a mistake for -oubash; Am prints the latter without comment.

[44]Am reasonably suggests -seira (Gk seiran) for the unattested Coptic siha. According to LSJ 1588B(I3), a seira was "a cord with a noose, like the lasso, used by the Sagartians and Sarmatians to entangle and drag away their enemies"; see Herodotus *Histories* 7.85. In the LXX (Prov 5:22), the rope is used metaphorically of sin, a use adopted by Origen and Chrysostom (see Lampe, 1227B).

[45]-diabathra (Gk), a ladder, ship's gangway, staircase, bridge, or drawbridge (LSJ 344A), but the image is not clear.

heart like a silversmith's stamp, reproving you and making known to you one by one the deeds you have done: what time you did them, what season; when you did this or when you did that. Simply put, they are all shameful to you and cause you to be scorned in both worlds: with the inhabitants of heaven and with the inhabitants of earth, the place of fearful universal judgment. [130] All the saints and all the heavenly ranks will be in mourning and will groan over you when they behold the great fall that has taken place in you on account of the ugly deeds you have done.

"But our Lord Jesus Christ is merciful and full of compassion, for there is no repentance nor compassion nor anyone to hear you unless the Compassionate One of his own accord—he whose treasuries are filled with mercy and pity, he who can kill and make alive—descends to Hell and rises again [Amos 9:2], that is, our Lord Jesus Christ, the savior of our souls and bodies, who does not wish the death of a sinner so much as his conversion and life [Ezek 33:11, 1 Tim 2:4, 2 Pet 3:9]. Let us understand these things, brothers, and let us be wise from now on, seeing his love for humanity, just as formerly when he had pity and wept over Lazarus, beseeching his Father's goodness[46] while Mary and Martha, the sisters of the dead man, poured forth tears, and after four days he raised him from the dead [Jn 11:1–44]. Let us draw near to him through prayers and holy tears so he will have pity on us and raise our souls from the death of sin that we may live by his mercy."

Abba Macarius Teaches about Trust in God

10   [131] One time a brother asked Abba Macarius, "Tell me, my father, what is it to throw oneself down before God?"

Abba Macarius said to him, "It is written that our Lord did not speak to people except in parables [Mt 13:14]. So, if an irrational wild

---

[46]Literally: in the presence of his Father's goodness. Am suggests "(implorant) la bonté de son Père," which I have followed; see Jn 11:41b-42.

beast leaps upon a domesticated animal and stands over it with great ferocity so that the animal beneath it weakly cowers before it, all its strength and hope[47] depend on its master and it cries out in a loud voice, signaling to its master. If its master hears it, then he quickly takes pity on it and runs and helps it and saves it from being destroyed by the wild beast. If the master of this irrational animal takes pity on it and hurries until he saves it from the wild beast, then how much more is it true for us, the rational sheep of Christ's flock? If we put our faith in him, he will not allow the Enemy to do violence to us but will send his angel to us to save us from the Devil. Therefore, my children, throwing oneself down before God is when a person does not trust in his own strength alone but places his faith in the help of God, for it is he who saves us."

Abba Macarius Teaches about the Passions

11   [132] Again he asked him, "My father, how can a person be free[48] from the passions and be renewed in the Spirit?"

The old man said to him, "I will give you an analogy.[49] It is like a tunic: if it is torn, a patch is put on it until it is made new once again. The tunic can be compared to the body, torn by sin and pleasure. The patch is the repentance that our Lord Jesus Christ [gives] to us."

Abba Macarius Teaches about the Sweetness of Christ

12   This same brother again [asked] him, "My father, guide me concerning [what is] sweet and what is salty" [Jas 3:11].

---

[47] *Helpis* (Gk *elpis*) is the same word translated below as "faith."
[48] Coptic *er remhe* was used both of the freeing of slaves and of being made free through exorcism, either or both of which senses may be apposite here.
[49] *-ainigma*; see 1 Cor 13:12.

Abba Macarius [said] to him, "They say that if the mother of a small child places the child on the ground, she puts some kind of sweet in his hand for him to lick so he won't vex[50] his mother. The vexing can be likened to sin and pleasure while the sweet, on the other hand, represents our Lord Jesus Christ, the blessed name, the true pearl, for it is written in the Holy Gospel that the kingdom of heaven is like a merchant who is looking for precious jewels. Therefore, when he found a valuable jewel, he went and sold what he possessed and bought it. So he gave up what he owned, his heart's desires, and wanted only the precious stone, that is, our Lord Jesus Christ, king of kings and lord of lords" [Mt 13:45, 1 Tim 6:15, Rev 17:14].

Abba Macarius Speaks to Abba Poemen about the Sweetness of Heaven

13   [133] Abba Poemen said, "I was sitting one time with some brothers beside Abba Macarius. I said to him, 'My father, what work must a person do in order to acquire life for himself?'

"The old man said to me, 'I know that when I was a child in my father's house I used to observe that the old women and the young people were chewing something in their mouths so that it would sweeten the saliva in their throats and the bad breath of their mouths, sweetening and refreshing their liver and all their innards.[51] If something fleshly can so sweeten those who chew it and ruminate it, then how much more the food of life, the spring of salvation, the fount of living water, the sweet of all sweets, our Lord Jesus Christ! If the demons hear his glorious name blessed by our mouths, they vanish like smoke. This blessed name, if we persevere in it and ruminate on it, opens up the spirit, the charioteer of the soul and the

---

[50] *či chelmi*; Crum, 516B, gives the meaning as "unknown." Am translates "ne cause point d'embarras."

[51] The island of Chios produced the aromatic *masticha*, which could be used as a kind of chewing gum.

body, and drives[52] all thoughts of evil out of the immortal soul [134] and reveals to it heavenly things, especially him who is in heaven, our Lord Jesus Christ, king of kings and lord of lords [1 Tim 6:15, Rev 17:14], who gives heavenly rewards to those who seek him with their whole heart.'"[53]

When Abba Poemen heard these things from him about whom Christ bears witness ("The righteous Macarius stands today before my judgment seat"), they threw themselves at his feet with tears, and after he prayed over them, he dismissed them and they gave glory to our Lord Jesus Christ.[54]

Abba Macarius and the Healing of the Antelope's Young[55]

14 When Abba Macarius was speaking openly to the brothers, he said, "One time when I was in the wadi gathering palm branches, an

---

[52]"Drives" translates *čōrem* while "opens up" and "reveals" translates *čōrp.*

[53]This passage seems to point to an early form of the Jesus Prayer; see #34, 35, 41, 42, and 44. See also Greek *AP* Macarius the Great 19. For a discussion, see Antoine Guillaumont, "The Jesus Prayer Among the Monks of Egypt," *Eastern Churches Review,* 6 (1974): 66–71; and Lucien Regnault, "La prière continuelle 'monologistos' dans la littérature apophthegmatique," *Irénikon,* 47 (1974): 467–93. Another valuable discussion is Kallistos Ware, "The Origins of the Jesus Prayer: Diadochus, Gaza, Sinai," in Cheslyn Jones, Geoffrey Wainwright, Edward Yarnold, eds., *The Study of Spirituality* (New York: Oxford University Press, 1986), 175–184. For the later tradition of the Jesus Prayer in Coptic-Arabic tradition, see Lucien Regnault, "Quelques apophthegmes arabes sur la 'Prière de Jésus,'" *Irénikon,* 52 (1979): 344–55; Kari Vogt, "The Coptic Practice of the Jesus Prayer: A Tradition Revived," in Nelly Van Doorn-Harder and Kari Vogt, eds., *Between Desert and City: The Coptic Orthodox Church Today* (Oslo: Novus forlag, 1997), 111–20; and Mark N. Swanson, "'These Three Words Will Suffice': The 'Jesus Prayer' in Coptic Tradition," *Parole de l'Orient,* 25 (2000): 695–714. On the related issue of unceasing prayer, see Lucien Regnault, "La prière continuelle 'monologistos' dans la littérature apophtegmatique," *Irénikon,* 47 (1974): 467–93, reprinted in *Les Pères du désert à travers leur Apophtegmes* (Solesmes, 1987), 113–39. See also Gabriel Bunge, "'Priez sans cesse': aux origines de la prière hésychaste," *Studia Monastica,* 30 (1988): 7–16.

[54]The text telescopes Poemen's hearing and his telling of the story to his disciples, who upon hearing it threw themselves at his feet.

[55]See *LH* 18.27–28 (= *Life of Macarius of Alexandria* [Coptic Palladiana] 2 in the

antelope came up to me, tearing out its fur, weeping as though it
were a he-goat, its tears flowing to the ground. It threw itself down
on top of my feet and moistened them with its tears, and I sat down
and stroked its face and anointed it with my hands, amazed at its
tears, while it gazed back at me.[56] After a while, it took hold of my
tunic and pulled on me. I followed it through the power of our Lord
Jesus Christ and when it took me to where it lived, I found its three
young [135] lying there. When I sat down, it took hold of them one
by one and placed them in my lap and when I touched them I found
that they were deformed: their chins were on their backs. I took pity
on them as their mother wept; I groaned over them, saying, 'You who
care for all of creation, our Lord Jesus Christ, who have numerous
treasuries of mercy, take pity on the creature you made.' After I said
these words accompanied by tears before my Lord Jesus Christ, I
stretched out my hand and made the saving sign of the cross over
the antelope's young, and they were healed. When I put them down,
their mother immediately gave them her attention. They went
underneath to her nipples and sucked her milk. She rejoiced over
them, delighting[57] in them, looking into my eyes with great joy. I
marveled at the goodness of God and the love for humanity of our
Lord Jesus Christ as shown by his tender mercies for me and for the
other beasts that he cares about. I got up and walked, giving glory
for the great goodness of our Lord Jesus Christ and the multitude of
his mercies for every creature he has made."

companion volume to this one, *Four Desert Fathers*) and *Historia Monachorum*
21.15–16 for a similar story about a hyena.

[56]Female goats bleat "longingly" during mating season; he-goats bleat even
more, and their bleating is like wailing of a sort. Driven to frenzy by rut, he-goats leave
their flock and wander from flock to flock in search of mates. To weep like a he-goat
is to weep pathetically, to give every evidence of being forlorn. The antelope's actions
here also resemble those of mourning humans; see *Iliad* 18.28–34, 19.282–90. I wish to
thank Apostolos N. Athanassakis for his suggestions here.

[57]-*holj*, which also means "to be sweet"; sweetness is an important word in the
Macarian corpus.

Abba Macarius Speaks about the Devastation of Scetis (AP Macarius 5)

15   Abba Macarius spoke to the brothers about the devastation of Scetis. [136] When they asked him about it, he said to them, "If you see cells built in the wadi and if you see trees planted near their doors, if you see lots of boys, gather your skins and flee."[58]

Abba Macarius Speaks about the Devastation and Renewal of Scetis

16   Some old men inquired of Abba Macarius, "What is the work of Scetis?"

He said to them, "It resembles and is like the four towns that God separated out for the children of Israel so that if an adulterer or murderer fled inside one of them he would be safe if he remained [there]" [Num 35:11].[59]

Again Abba Macarius said to them, "There are towns that the king of kings and lord of lords [Rev 17:14], Christ our God, founded and made strong, and he gathered together from the four corners of the earth spiritual soldiers and had them dwell there, appointing for them laws and commandments, and he said to them, 'Do these things and I will make the kings of the earth bow their heads to you.' And when they heard him, they did just as he had commanded them, and these things will happen up to the time of the first destruction of Scetis forty years from now because they have satisfied all their passions.[60]

[58]There may be a play on words here: "boys" is -*alōoui* while "gather" is *alioui*.

[59]The reference is to the "cities of refuge" established in ancient Israel, commanded in Numbers 35 and fulfilled in Joshua 20. There were, however, six biblical cities, not four. "Four" may be an assimilation to the "four corners of the earth" in the next par. or it may be an allusion to the four "congregations" (Cassian's term) of Scetis, seen as refuges.

[60]The first destruction of Scetis at the hands of barbarian marauders took place in 407–8, which would date the telling of this saying (either in history or tradition) to 367–68.

"Once again Christ the King will have pity on them and will bring them back a second time [137] and once again he will lay down these laws and commandments, saying, 'Do these. Just as I did with your fathers I will do with you.' And they listened [*sic*] and kept half of these commandments. These things will take place up to the second destruction of Scetis on account of the numerous comforts they allowed themselves.[61]

"And once again Christ the King, to whom the Church universal offers worship, remembered their fathers and he will bring them back once again a third time and will bring them these same laws and commandments once again and they will say to him, 'It is not possible for us to keep them.' Christ the King will not wish to destroy the towns and he will say to them, 'Dwell only in the towns and I will do with you as I did with your fathers and I will visit you. If I come and find that I am dwelling with you and you with me, then I and my good Father and the Holy Spirit Paraclete[62] will build us a dwelling place among you in order for you to glorify us for ever without end.' "

Abba Macarius Tells Abba Evagrius about Free Will

17   While Abba Poemen was sitting beside him along with Abba Paphnutius,[63] the true and faithful disciple, Abba Evagrius asked Abba Macarius about the purity of free will.[64]

[138] Abba Macarius told them, "The purity of free will is the person who will give a thousand silver coins to obtain what he wants

---

[61]The second destruction of Scetis took place in 434. On both destructions, see Evelyn White, 2.154–5 and 161.

[62]On these terms, see #5 above.

[63]In *AP* Macarius 28 and 37 Paphnutius is described as "the disciple of Abba Macarius"; in the *Life of Macarius of Scetis* 36, he is described as "the holy man Abba Paphnutius, who was the greatest of the saint's disciples. It was he who assumed the fatherhood in the holy places after Abba Macarius." See #65, 74 below.

[64]-*prohairesis*.

through his own free will, and these coins will be like a single copper coin to him. If his free will acts so forcefully on account of a single copper coin, he will suffer the loss of one thousand gold coins on account of the force of his free will."[65]

They said to him, "What do these words mean?"

Abba Macarius said to them, "Search and see. Examine my words."

And when they examined his words, they found them to be true, and after they asked his forgiveness, he prayed over them and dismissed them while they gave glory to our Lord Jesus Christ.

Abba Macarius Lists the Monastic Virtues[66]

18   Abba Macarius said, "When you get up in the morning each day, make it the beginning of your life as a monk: practice every virtue and every commandment of God; fearfully practice perseverance and patience; demonstrate a love of God and a love of people with a humble heart and bodily humility, with mourning and the distress of being [139] confined in prison, with prayers and supplications and groans, with purity of tongue while humbly guarding your eyes, without anger, in peace, without returning evil to an evildoer, without passing judgment on those in need, without thinking of yourself in anything, placing yourself below every creature; with renunciation of material things and fleshly things, with the struggle of the cross, with spiritual poverty, with good free will and bodily asceticism, with fasting and repentance and tears, with the combat war brings and returning from imprisonment, with pure counsel and the tasting of good goodness, quietly at midday; with manual

---

[65]See perhaps Mt 11:12 where the violent take the kingdom of God by force.

[66]This saying is extremely close to *AP* John Kolobos 34 and it is clearly an example of a saying handed down with multiple attributions. The Greek Systematic Apophthegmata I.13 also attributes the saying to John; see also I.16, which is given to Macarius.

work, with vigils, with numerous prayers, with hunger and thirst, with frost and nakedness and afflictions and the acquisition of your tomb as though you had already been placed in it, placing your death near you day after day, lost in the deserts and mountains and holes of the earth" [Heb 11:38].

Abba Macarius Speaks about Giving Birth in the Spirit

19   Our father Abba Macarius again said, "It is written, 'Your fear, Lord, we conceived; we were in labor and gave birth to a spirit of salvation' [Is 26:18 (LXX)].[67] See [140] that you grasp what I am saying and not be someone who does not give birth. To be sure, my brothers, these are matters of the marriage chamber [Mt 22:11], but they are also the fruits of those who have done their work well [Mt 25:20–22], those who have built their house on solid rock [Mt 7:24]: compassion, and faith. Lord, let us not be lacking in your fear and wrath and let us not lack humility and mourning. Take heed of these things, which are salvation in our Lord, you who wish to live in peace. Amen."

Abba Macarius Talks about the Meaning of the Mustard Seed

20   Some brothers were sitting around Abba Macarius and openly asked him about the mustard seed: "What is its interpretation" [Mt 13:31//Lk 13:19; Mt 17:20//Lk 17:6]?

He told them, "The mustard seed can be compared to the spirit,[68] for if a person possesses knowledge of our Lord Jesus Christ, it is said about him that his spirit is subtle. Just as the mustard seed is subtle and seasoned, in the same way it is said that the teacher is seasoned and his understanding is subtle."

[67]By way of contrast, see Job 15:35, Ps 7:14, and Jas 1:15.
[68]Nous.

Abba Macarius Explains the Parable Further

21   The brothers said to him, "What is growth? What are our herbs" [Mt 13:32]?

Abba Macarius said to them, "Growth is the spiritual virtues; the herbs are the ‹innocent›,[69] the pure, and the simple. A tree exists so [141] the birds of heaven can come and nest there in its branches [Lk 13:19]. May we too be found to be heavenly beings! Now the tree is the teacher who teaches; the lessons and the encouragement that he gives his students are the branches. The mustard seed has within it but a single heart; my brothers, may we too be a single heart within our Lord Jesus Christ and be one in virtue, that we may receive the leaven [1 Cor 5:6, Gal 5:9], that is, the grace of our Lord Jesus Christ, which we have hidden in the three measures [Mt 13:33]: the soul and the body and the spirit. The three measures comprise a single human being, perfect and complete [1 Th 5:23], a measure of the full stature of our Lord Jesus Christ [Eph 4:13]. All these things our Lord Jesus Christ spoke in numerous parables and he did not speak to people without using parables" [Mt 13:34].

When the brothers heard these things, they marveled at the subtlety and fineness of his mind and their hearts were made new so that what is written was fulfilled concerning them: "In my meditation a fire will burn" [Ps 38:4 (LXX)].

Three Sayings

22A   Abba Macarius said, "Let us not slacken our resolve nor [142] be without hope, for with every breath that we take our Lord Jesus Christ gives us opportunity for repentance."

22B   He also said, "Just as when the smith's anvil is struck every day it becomes pure, so it is with a person who submits himself to mor-

[69]Codex: -*akeros*, which Am corrects, incorrectly, to -*akairos* ("importunate"); it should be -*akeraios* ("innocent").

tifications, being taught each day, who receives teaching and keeps watch over it: he is pure and is protected from the hidden ambush of the Evil One."

22C He also said, "Let us not cause that fountain to bubble up which is salty because of its single source, that is, the well of the heart, but let bubble up without ceasing that which is sweet all the time, that is, our Lord Jesus Christ" [James 3:11].

Abba Macarius Teaches about Repentance and Christ's Love

23   A brother asked Abba Macarius, "My father, I have committed a transgression."[70]

Abba Macarius said to him, "It is written, my child, 'I do not desire the death of a sinner so much as his repentance and his life' [Ezek 33:11, 1 Tim 2:4, 2 Pet 3:9]. Repent,[71] therefore, my child; you will see him who is gentle, our Lord Jesus Christ, his face full of joy for you, like a nursing mother whose face is full of joy for her child. When he raises his hands and his face up to her, even if he is full of all kinds of uncleanness, she does not turn away from that bad smell and excrement[72] [143] but takes pity on him and lifts him up and presses him to her breast, her face full of joy, and everything about him is sweet to her. If, then, this created person has pity for her child, how much greater is the love of the creator, our Lord Jesus Christ, for us!

[70]Literally: I have fallen into a transgression. "To fall" is an important concept in early monastic spirituality. Although the monk does not ask a question, the text uses -*shen* (*shini*), the verb ordinarily used for questions. "What do I do?" may be supplied.

[71]Both "repentance" (-*tastho*-) and "repent" (*kot*-) in Coptic convey the idea of (re)turning, turning back, as in Latin *convertere.*

[72]*Nilahōj.* Crum, 150A, cites this passage and says the meaning is unknown; I have followed Am's translation, which Regnault and Guillaumont also follow.

Abba Macarius Teaches about Repentance

24   A brother asked Abba Macarius, "Tell me the meaning of repentance."

Abba Macarius said to him, "Repentance does not consist only of kneeling, like the divining rod that indicates water by going up and down, but is like a wise goldsmith who wishes to craft a chain: with a link of gold and a link of silver, even with iron and lead, he lengthens the chain until he completes his work. This too is the form that repentance takes. All the virtues depend on it.

Abba Macarius Teaches about Pity and Compassion

25   Some brothers asked Abba Macarius the Great, "Are feelings of pity more important than works?"

He said to them, "Yes."

The brothers said to him, "Persuade us."

When Abba Macarius saw that they were fearful and timid, wanting to gladden them he said to them, "Look at the street vendor who sells to a customer. He says to him, 'I've given you a good deal,' but if he sees that the customer is unhappy, he gives [144] him back a little of his money and the customer goes away happy. It's the same with acts also: if they stand unhappy before God, the giver of good things, the true judge, our Lord Jesus Christ, his numerous acts of compassion move him and the acts leave with joy and rejoicing and gladness."

When the brothers heard these things, they were encouraged, and when Abba Macarius saw that they were gladdened, he spoke to them again with joy: "A small quantity of oil gladdens a person's face in the presence of the king of this world; in the same way, may a little virtue gladden the soul in the presence of the king of those who dwell in heaven and those who dwell on earth, our Lord Jesus Christ, who possesses numerous treasuries of mercy, for it is written, 'From the days of John the Baptist up to now, the kingdom of heaven is taken by force and some who are violent seize it' [Mt 11:12]. So, then, let us too use a little force in exchange for the kingdom of heaven; we will seize for ourselves him who is king forever, our Lord Jesus Christ."

When the brothers heard these things, they threw themselves down and prostrated themselves at his feet. They left him rejoicing and giving glory to our Lord Jesus Christ.

Abba Macarius Teaches about Mercy

26 [145] A brother asked Abba Macarius, "I want to know: how is acting mercifully powerful?"

Abba Macarius said to him, "If the king banishes some men to a foreign and distant country, one of them acquires wisdom and counsel from those in authority; he grows powerful and sends gifts to that king, but the others do not do likewise. After a long time the king sends for those men and has them returned to their city and country. Will not the one who sent presents to the king rejoice more than the others because he will be made their champion? Will he not find greater freedom of speech than those who sent nothing at all? Does a commander-in-chief not have freedom of speech before the king of this world? So it is with mercy before Christ, the great king: it has great freedom of speech before him and offers a defense against everyone who accuses it.[73]

Abba Macarius Teaches about the Soul

27 This same brother asked about this reading: "So that your youth is renewed like the eagle's" [Ps 103:5].

---

[73]In other words, mercy covers a multitude of sins; see Jas 2:13.

Abba Macarius said to him, "If gold is heated in the fire, it becomes [146] new. It's the same with the soul: if she is virtuous and is purified of all her impurities and imperfections, she will be renewed and will fly to the heights."

Further Teaching about the Soul

28 The brother inquired further: "What is this 'flying to the heights,' my father?"

Abba Macarius said to him, "If the eagle flies up to the heights of the air, he escapes from the hunter's trap; if, on the other hand, he comes down, he falls into the hunter's snares. Thus it is with the soul: if she is negligent and descends from the heights of virtue, she falls into the snares of the spiritual hunter."

Abba Macarius Teaches about Constancy in God

29 The brother inquired again, "Tell me about constancy in God, my father."

Abba Macarius said to him, "It is like the honeybee flying in the midst of the green plants and the flowers of the field, sucking honey until it fills its hive with what it has gathered: unless someone smokes out the hive, it cannot be robbed of its sweetness."

The brother said to him, "What is the smoke and what is the sweetness, my father?"

The old man said to him, "Acts of fornication and defilements and abominations and pollutions and envious thoughts and hatreds and vain imaginings [147] and the remaining pleasures: these are the smoke. The flowers on the other hand are the virtues; the bee is the worship of God; the hive is the heart; the sweetness itself is our Lord Jesus Christ. Therefore, the person who shows constancy and who fills his soul with all the virtues and with all purity is the one who demonstrates constancy in God. Go, my child."

Abba Macarius Teaches about Fornication and Avarice

30   A brother asked Abba Macarius, "My thoughts reproach me, saying, 'Be first to church.' "[74]

Abba Macarius said to him, "You are speaking about the gate of heaven [Gen 28:17] and the mother of all living things [Gen 3:20]. I say to you, my child: Watch for the acceptable time, watch for the day of salvation [2 Cor 6:2] when you leave behind the works of the Devil, for there is coming a day when many will be prevented from entering the church and they will become strangers to the mysteries because, out of fear, they will be caught in the grasp of what rules that time. Their mouths are open like the sardine[75] in the ocean; they gather together large amounts of money like the ant that gathers during the days of summer. I say to you, my child, that every evil act arises from fornication and the love of money, these two things. Although fornication is more evil, it is only a temporary thing, and a person turns his nose up at it and spits on it on account of its bad smell, [148] but avarice exists to acquire; it becomes sweet to you, for it is insatiable. It will be necessary, therefore, to put a seal on the doors of the church in the desert and on the mouths of the dead out of fear of what will rule at that time, for some will arise who will search and seek out inheritances from those who are asleep and they will forget what is written: 'If riches come, do not set your heart on them' [Ps 62:10]. This is also what the apostle says about riches: 'The root of all evil is the love of money' [1 Tim 6:10]. Now, then, my child, fight with all your might, for Abba Antony said, 'It is right that each person become his own church at this time,'[76] that is, it is right for each person to use all his power to purify his soul, the church of God, so that with a quiet voice we may send on high a trinitarian hymn to our Lord God through the firm confession of the orthodox faith."

[74]"What shall I do" may be supplied. See n. 70 above.
[75]I am taking *sardi* to equal Gk *sardinē*.
[76]I have not been able to locate this saying.

Abba Macarius Receives Power from Christ

31   It was said about our father Saint Abba Macarius the Great that when he advanced in virtue he received power to intercede[77] with our Lord Jesus Christ; as a result, the hostile spirits were upset and [149] trembled in his presence on account of the intercessory power that was with him.[78]

Apa Shenoute Marvels at the Works of the Monks of Scetis

32   At the time when the wise Cyril summoned Saint Apa[79] Shenoute to the holy synod that met in Ephesus concerning the impious human-worshipper Nestorius, our Lord Jesus Christ gave them friendly assistance until they subscribed to the deposition of that despicable person.[80] After this battle waged by Saint Cyril and the holy synod of bishops, they wished to return to their episcopal sees as commanded by the godly emperor Theodosius, and Saint Apa Shenoute was taken up into a cloud. When it carried him over

[77]-*paraklēton*, that is, of the Paraclete, so other possible infinitives are "to comfort," "console," "exhort," and "advocate."

[78]On hostile spirits, see Jean Daniélou, "Les démons de l'air dans la Vie d'Antoine," in Basilius Steidle, ed., *Antonius Magnus Eremita, 356–1956: Studia ad Antiquum Monachismum Spectantia* (Studia Anselmiana, 38; Rome: Herder, 1956), 136–147. On the monk as patron, see especially Peter Brown, "The Rise and Function of the Holy Man in Late Antiquity," *Journal of Roman Studies,* 61 (1971): 80–101; reprinted in Brown, *Society and the Holy in Late Antiquity* (Berkeley: University of California Press, 1982), 103–52; "The Rise and Function of the Holy Man in Late Antiquity: 1971–1997," *Journal of Early Christian Studies,* 6.3 (1998): 353–376; "The Saint as Exemplar in Late Antiquity," in John Stratton Hawley, ed., *Saints and Virtues* (Berkeley: University of California Press, 1987).

[79]The text switches from "Abba" to "Apa" for Shenoute throughout this paragraph.

[80]Shenoute (385–465), founder of the White and Red monasteries, accompanied Cyril, archbishop of Alexandria (d. 444), to the Council of Ephesus in 431. Nestorius (d. 451) was condemned for advocating two Persons in Christ. See Aloys Grillmeier, in collaboration with Theresia Hainthaler, *Christ in Christian Tradition,* 2.4 (Engl. ed.; London: Mowbray, 1996), 167–234.

the holy place of our father, the righteous Abba Macarius the Great of Scetis (he to whom the voice of the Lord had come, saying, "You have become a god upon the earth,"[81] and who saw in a vision the holy prayers of his children becoming like the sweet smoke of incense going to the throne of the Almighty), the old man, the archimandrite Apa Shenoute, marveled to himself, saying, "When my Lord Jesus Christ sets me down in my monastery, I will come to this place to see its [150] work and those who live in it in order to see what sort of people they are."

After he greeted the brothers in his monastery, he took with him some of the elders and went to Scetis to the holy place of Abba Macarius and the superior at that time received him with joy and with open and loving encouragement. Saint Apa Shenoute thought to himself, "According to the vision I saw when I was mounted on the cloud, works like this are not attainable."

While Saint Apa Shenoute was pondering thoughts like this within himself, God revealed his thoughts to the holy superior of the monastery, and since he wanted the monastery to profit from Apa Shenoute's visit, he walked through the monastery with him. Therefore, with the superior accompanying him, the old men of the monastery received a blessing from Apa Shenoute. Then the superior took Apa Shenoute to where the brothers cooked their meals. A small feast was taking place that day for one of the faithful. In his impatience, the brother who tended the fire under the kettle allowed it to boil over, and the superior said to him, "Thrust your forearm into the kettle, my child, and turn the meat." In obedience he thrust his forearm into the kettle and turned the food.

[151] When Saint Apa Shenoute saw this great wonder (the brother was not harmed at all), he publicly said, "Truly, the name 'without work' will not be able to divide a people, for works raised up Tabitha; in the same way, because of the pure works of Abba Macarius, faith has raised the dead [Acts 9:36–42].[82] And what shall

[81]See *Virtues* 1 above and n. 16 there.
[82]Tabitha (Dorcas in Greek) was raised from the dead by Peter.

I say about *my* children? Indeed, their eyes have flowed with tears and they have constricted their stomachs on account of their severe diet, and up to now they have demonstrated no power like this."

And so he went to his monastery, giving profit to the place, and giving glory to our Lord Jesus Christ and his servant, Abba Macarius the righteous."

Abba Macarius Explains a Saying by Abba Sisoës

33　A brother asked Abba Macarius, "What does this word that Abba Sisoës said mean: 'There is one who receives ten while giving one'?"

He responded and said to him, "Since the Devil, either by night or by day, never ceases taking aim at the combatant and the ascetic who practices abstinence, if he in turn resists the Devil with just one blow (that is, with tears, throwing himself down before the goodness and mercy of our Lord [152] Jesus Christ), may he who loves those who are good, our true God, rejoice over that one blow and bring to naught the ten blows of the Devil, because man is merely flesh and blood. With a single blow, however, he has defeated the works of the incorporeal one: it is the Devil's practice to fall before humility, the help that our Lord Jesus Christ protects us with through his holy grace."[83]

Abba Macarius Teaches about Ruminating on the Name of Christ

34　The brother again asked, "What work is best for the ascetic and the abstinent?"

He responded and said to him, "Blessed is the person who will be found tending[84] the blessed name of our Lord Jesus Christ with-

[83]See *AP* Poemen 88 for, apparently, a much condensed version.
[84]-*amoni* means both "to be in possession of" and "to pasture, feed, tend cattle."

out ceasing and with contrition of heart.[85] Of all the ascetic practices, none is better than this blessed nourishment if you ruminate on it at all times like the sheep: the sheep regurgitates and savors the sweet taste of its cud[86] until it enters the interior of its heart and brings sweetness and good fatness to its intestines and to all its innards. Do you not see how beautiful its cheeks are, filled with the sweet cud [153] that it ruminates in its mouth? May our Lord Jesus Christ also bless us with his sweet and fat name!"

Abba Macarius Explains the Above Saying

35   A brother asked Abba Macarius, "Tell me the meaning of this saying, 'the meditation of my heart is placed before you'" [Ps 19:14, 49:3].

The old man said to him, "There is no better meditation than having this saving and blessed name of our Lord Jesus Christ continually within you, as it is written: 'Like a swallow I will call and like a dove I will meditate' [Is 38:14 (LXX)]. Thus it is with the person who worships God by tending the saving name of our Lord Jesus Christ."

Abba Macarius Explains the Meaning of the Wolf

36   It was said about Abba Macarius the Great that one time when he was working the harvest with the brothers,[87] a wolf opened its mouth and let out a great cry, its eyes staring up to heaven to the Lord. The saint stopped and smiled with tears in his eyes.

[85]See #13 above and the note there on the Jesus Prayer; see #35, 41, 42, and 44 below.

[86]"Cud" and "ruminate" are nominative and verbal forms of the same word in Coptic.

[87]Apparently a common practice; see *AP* Macarius 7.

When the brothers saw him, they were amazed. They threw themselves down at his feet, beseeching him, "We beseech you, our father, tell us why you were staring with tears in your eyes."

While he stared with tears in his eyes, his face shone like fire, like the rays of the sun, on account of the grace [154] of our Lord Jesus Christ that was in him. He said to them, "Didn't you hear what this wolf cried out?"

They said to him, "What was that, our father?"

He said to them, "He cried up to the lover of humanity, to the compassionate one alone, who possesses the treasuries of numerous mercies, our Lord Jesus Christ, saying, 'If you are not going to care about me and provide me with my food, at least tell me why I am suffering. You were the one who created me.' If even flesh-eating beasts have understanding and cry up to the goodness of our Lord Jesus Christ and he nourishes all of them, then how will he not care about us, who are rational beings, with his bountiful mercy and compassion?"

[88]As the luminary and light-giver was saying these things to the brothers, the wolf stood with its mouth agape.[89] Afterwards, the beast went to the place where God had prepared food for it and all the brothers prostrated themselves and venerated the holy feet of our righteous father, the Spiritbearer Abba Macarius the Great, giving glory to our Lord Jesus Christ.

Abba Macarius Advises Two Brothers Who Want to Live Together

37   [155] It was said about Abba Macarius the Great that an old man paid him a visit along with a brother. They said to him, "We wish to live together as one, our father."

---

[88]In the margin it says, "Start here. Begin with the ?th Sunday of Lent." The number seems to be missing

[89]There may be a play on words here: "wolf" is *-ouōnsh* in Coptic while "with its mouth agape" (or "astonished") is *-onsh.* The more usual verb for astonishment, *er shpēr,* is used earlier with the brothers.

Abba Macarius said to the old man, "First be like a shepherd. If the ox-fly[90] sows worms in the sheep, he gives it medicine until he kills the worms, but if the sheep shows an infestation he uses an unguent[91] on it until he removes the infestation."

The old man said to him, "Tell me the meaning of this saying."

Abba Macarius said to him, "The ox-fly is like the Devil while the sheep is like the brother who lives with you. The worms are the passions and the pleasures of the demons who dwell in the soul and breed in the heart, like the worms that live in the wounds of the body; the medicine that wipes out the infestation is progress[92] and abstinence and the saving teaching of God. These are the things that purify the soul, cleansing it of all passion and every evil of the wicked enemies that the demons send against us."

He also spoke to the brother: "My son, be like Isaac, who obeyed his father until he took him up high as a sacrifice and an offering acceptable before God [See Gen 22]; he has become enrolled[93] in the Church [156] until the end of the ages with the glory of our Lord Jesus Christ."

Christ the Compassionate Potter

38   Abba Macarius also said, "The potter who sits working the earth first takes care to fashion vessels decorated with colorful motifs that become honored at the morning and evening meals of emperors and are even honored by the priestly order of the Church. After making these, he fashions other vessels that are ugly and inferior [Rom 9:21, 2 Tim 2:20] for use as chamber pots and for birthing stools for the newborn and innocent. After making these, he loads the furnace and

---

[90]*Serphōt*, which occurs only here; Crum, 356B, suggests "insect (?)." I have followed Am ("taon"), as do Regnault and Guillaumont.

[91]*čabōt*. Crum, 806A, is also not certain about this word.

[92]*Prokopē* was an important monastic virtue.

[93]Coptic *egkraphon* = Gk *eggraphon*; see Lampe, 398B.

fires them. Truly,[94] I say that just as he prays for the precious and decorated vessels, he also prays for those that are ugly and inferior because they are works of his hand.

"It is the same with our Lord Jesus Christ, who possesses the treasuries of numerous mercies, who alone is compassionate with his good Father and the Holy Spirit: just as he rejoices over the person who is honored and adorned with the pure progress of virtue and abstinence, [157] he also rejoices over the conversion of someone who is inferior, that is, the sinner, as it is written, 'There will be rejoicing in heaven in the presence of the angels of God over one sinner, if he repents' [Lk 15:7]. He also said, 'I do not desire the death of the sinner so much as his conversion and his life' [Ezek 33:11, 1 Tim 2:4, 2 Pet 3:9]. When he took on this flesh, he also willingly accepted its griefs. On account of this, our Lord Jesus Christ also says, 'I have not come to invite the righteous to repentance but sinners' " [Mt 9:13].

Abba Evagrius Speaks of Abba Macarius

39   Abba Evagrius said, "I visited Abba Macarius and said to him, 'Tell me a word so I may live.'

"He said to me, 'If I speak to you, will you listen and do it?'

"I said to him, 'My faith and my love are not hidden from you.'

"Abba Macarius said to me, 'Truly, I lack the adornment[95] of virtue; you, however, are good. But if you cast off the pridefulness of this world's rhetoric and clothe yourself in the humility of the tax collector [Lk 18: 9–14], you will live.'

"When he said these things to me, all my thoughts dissipated, and when I asked his forgiveness he prayed over me and dismissed me. And I walked and found fault with myself, saying, [158] 'My thoughts were not hidden from Abba Macarius, the man of God,

---

[94]*Amēn*, as in the Gospel of John.
[95]*Solsel* is a homonym, meaning both "adornment" and "consolation."

and every time I go to meet with him I tremble on account of his ability to make me listen and it's a humbling experience for me."

Abba Macarius Interprets a Brother's Saying

40 It was said concerning Abba Macarius that when he was passing through Egypt one time with some brothers he heard one of them lamenting and saying, "An Alexandria of rock fell on me and I didn't die; a hut of reeds fell on me and I died."

The old man was astonished at these words and when the brothers saw his astonishment, they threw themselves at his feet, beseeching him and saying, "Tell us, our father, the meaning of these words."

He said to them, "There is a great mystery in these words, my children. The rock is like our Lord Jesus Christ, as it is written concerning him:[96] 'The rock that the lawbreaking Jews scorned has become the corner capital' [Ps 118:22; see Mt 21:42//Mk 12:10//Lk 20:17; Acts 4:11, Eph 2:20], which has come about because of the Lord and is astonishing to our eyes [Ps 118:23]. This, moreover, is the true stone of great value for which the merchant paid all his heart's desire [Mt 13:46]. He took this rock into the inner chambers of his heart and found it—that is, our Lord Jesus Christ—sweeter than honey and the honeycomb [Ps 19:10]. [159] The person who will safeguard this stone that is in his heart will receive great recompense in the glory of our Lord Jesus Christ in the kingdom of heaven forever. Our Lord Jesus Christ has made his face like a sharp rock, according to the word of the apostle when he says, 'The rock is Christ' [1 Cor 10:4]. He gave his back to the whip and his cheeks to slaps [Is 53:5], but for us and for our salvation he did not turn his face away from the shame of being spat upon. And if our Lord Jesus Christ now sits on us[97] in our weaknesses on account of his great love for us, the soul is immortal on account of the pure passionlessness within the heart.

[96]Or: it (the rock).
[97]That is, like the "Alexandria of rock" the brother spoke about above.

The Devil, however, is powerless, like the reed, and if he falls on a person and uses force on him and tyrannizes him, if the person does not heed him and does not cry out to the goodness of God but instead falls in with the passions of the Devil, the Spirit of God withdraws from him.[98] Then the soul, since it is in the body, dies on account of the drunkenness of the passions and their stench."

Abba Macarius Teaches about Relying upon the Name of Christ

41   [160] Abba Macarius the Great said, "Concentrate on this name of our Lord Jesus Christ with a contrite heart, the words welling up from your lips and drawing you to them. And do not depict him with an image in your mind but concentrate on calling to him: 'Our Lord Jesus, have mercy on me.'[99] Do these things in peace and you will see the peace of his divinity within you; he will run off the darkness of the passions that dwell within you and he will purify the inner person [2 Cor 4:16, Eph 3:16] just as Adam was pure in paradise. This is the blessed name that John the Evangelist pronounced: 'Light of the world and unending sweetness, the food of life and the true food'" [Jn 6:48, 6:55, 8:12].

Abba Macarius Teaches Abba Evagrius to Call upon the Name of Christ

42   Abba Evagrius said, "I visited Abba Macarius, distressed by my thoughts and the passions of the body. I said to him, 'My father, tell me a word so I may live.'

"Abba Macarius said to me, 'Bind the ship's cable to the mooring anvil and through the grace of our Lord Jesus Christ the ship will pass through[100] the diabolical waves and tumults of this murky sea and the deep darkness of this vain world.'

[98]See #5 above.
[99]This is part of the Jesus Prayer; see #13, 34, and 35 above and 42 and 44 below.
[100]There may be a play on words here: "pass through" is *-sen* and "bind" is *senh.*

"I said to him, 'What is the ship? What is [161] the ship's cable? What is the mooring anvil?'

"Abba Macarius said to me, 'The ship is your heart. Guard it. The ship's cable is your spirit; bind it to our Lord Jesus Christ, who is the mooring anvil that prevails over all the tumults and diabolical waves that fight against the saints. For it is not easy to say with each breath, "Lord Jesus, have mercy on me. I bless you, my Lord Jesus." If you are distressed by people and the misfortunes of this world, say "My Lord Jesus, help me."[101] The fish swallows the waves and will be ensnared in them and will not know it. But when we persevere in the saving name of our Lord Jesus Christ, he, through the things he does for us, will ensnare the Devil by his nostrils [Job 40:26][102] and we will know our weakness, because our help is in our Lord Jesus Christ' " [Ps 124:8].

Abba Macarius Tells a Parable about Compassion

43   One time Abba Macarius told this parable when the brothers asked him about pity. The old man said to them, "There was a pitiless ruler in a town and one year a famine took place in that town so that the people despaired and thought they would die. A man approached this ruler and asked for bread because of the hunger in his belly and, on account of his impudence toward that pitiless ruler [Lk 18:5], with numerous scornful words and causing great suffering, [162] the ruler gave the man bread, but not without causing his blood to flow. This was the day of the dormition of her who brought our Lord Jesus Christ into the world for us, Mary the holy Mother of God. That very night, while that pitiless ruler was still asleep,[103] his soul was suddenly taken away from his body and he was dragged

---

[101]See *AP* Macarius the Great 19 (Ward, 131).

[102]Gregory of Nyssa somewhere uses the image of God, by means of Christ's sacrifice, snaring the Devil by his nostrils.

[103]"Asleep" and "dormition" share the same root: *-nkot.*

away to be cast into bitter torments in order to be punished, and while he was being pitilessly dragged, a voice came from him who possesses numerous treasuries of mercy and compassion, he who alone is compassionate, our lord Jesus Christ, our true God, he who blots out sins and forgives iniquities, saying, 'Return this soul to its body because this man gave bread to the man suffering from hunger and especially because today is the dormition of her who brought me into the world, the Virgin Mary.'[104]

"When that man awakened from death, he remembered the voice he had heard when he was being dragged to punishments and he said, 'On account of a single loaf of bread that I gave that man—and I did it in anger and even caused blood to flow from him—my Lord Jesus Christ has brought me out from bitter punishments. If I had distributed all my possessions, how much more would I have profited!' [163] So he distributed his possessions even more, even so far as to also include his body, which he sold into slavery[105] and gave the price to the poor[106] and the weak. Because of that man's love for other people and his upright intentions, he was invited into the priestly rank of the Church so that he was worthy of the episco-

---

[104]The date would be 21 Tobi (16 January). On the Dormition of Mary, see Michel van Esbroeck, "La dormition chez les coptes," *Actes du IVe Congrès Copte, Louvain-la-Neuve, 5–10 sept. 1988*, ed. M. Rassart-Debergh et J. Ries (Publications de l'Institut Orientaliste de Louvain, 41; Louvain-la-Neuve: Institut Orientaliste, 1992), 436–45; repr. in van Esbroeck, *Aux origines de la Dormition de la Vierge: Etudes historiques sur les traditions orientales* (Collected Studies Series, 472; Aldershot: Variorum, 1995), XI.436–45. Van Esbroeck notes, 436, that the Copts divided the feast of the Assumption into the Dormition on 21 Tobi (16 January) and the Ascension on 16 Mesori (9 August). He does not include the *Virtues* in the list of documents on 436–37. See also Brian E. Daley, *On the Dormition of Mary: Early Patristic Homilies* (Crestwood, N.Y.: St. Vladimir's Seminary Press, 1998). An apophthegm from the Anonymous Collection, N599, attributed to Paul the Simple, tells of a vision he had of a deceased disciple who had been condemned to punishment but was saved by the intercession of the Virgin Mary; see Lucien Regnault, *Les Sentences des pères du désert: série des anonymes* (Solesmes: Bellefontaine, 1985). On these types of stories, see Antonie Guillaumont, *Aux origines du monachisme chrétien* (Spiritualité Orientale, 30; Solesmes: Bellefontaine, 1979), 142.

[105]"Gave" and "sold" are the same verb in Coptic: *tēi*.

[106]"Poor" (*hēki*) and "hungry" (*hko*) share the same root in Coptic.

pacy and celebrated the liturgy, giving glory to our Lord Jesus Christ."

Abba Macarius Recounts a Visit He Made to an Old Man

44 Abba Macarius said, "I visited an old man who had taken to his bed with an illness, but the old man preferred to say the saving and blessed name of our Lord Jesus Christ. While I asked him about his health he joyfully said to me, 'While I was persevering in partaking of the sweet food of life of the holy name of our Lord Jesus Christ, I was seized with the sweetness of sleep. I saw in a vision Christ the King like a Nazirite [Num 6:2, Jdg 13:5, Mt 2:23][107] and he said to me three times, "See, see that it is I and no one besides me" [Is 45:18, 21–22]. Afterwards, I ‹burned›[108] with great joy for what is high and forgot the pain.' "

Abba Macarius Warns against Gluttony (Coptic Sayings 28)

45 [164] Abba Macarius said, "The person who will fill himself with bread and water has given the key to his house to thieves."

Abba Macarius Recognizes a Brother's Extraordinary Humility

46 It was said concerning a brother who lived in a monastery, who had another brother living in the monastery with him, that he stole some small pots from the storeroom of the steward of the monastery. The thief put the pots in a sack and deposited them with the brother who did not know that they were stolen but who thought

[107]In Gregory Nazianzus and Basil of Caesarea the word came to mean "ascetic"; see Lampe, 896B.

[108]Following Am's suggestion to read *moh* instead of the codex's *noh* ("shook").

they belonged to the thief. A little later the pots turned up missing and the monks searched each of the brothers' cells. They entered the cell of the brother with whom the pots had been deposited and searched for them and when they found them in his possession, he threw himself down and asked for forgiveness, saying, "I have become a laughingstock. I have sinned. Forgive me." And the brother who had stolen the pots and deposited them with the second brother heaped scorn on the brother in whose cell the pots were discovered and slapped him on the face, wishing to cast him out of the monastery, and in all these things the accused did not deny anything but even humbled himself before the first brother, saying, "I have sinned. Forgive me."

And the brother in whose cell the pots were found became the object of hatred of the priest[109] and of all the brothers in the monastery; the brother who stole the pots especially hated him [165] and reproached him every hour of the day, calling him a thief in front of the brothers.[110] After the accused had spent two years in the monastery, enduring this great reproach, afterwards God revealed the matter to Abba Macarius in Scetis and Abba Macarius went to Egypt[111] in order to see the brother. When he drew near the monastery, all the brothers gathered together with palm branches in order to stand before Abba Macarius [Jn 12:12–13]. [. . .][112] The accused also replied, saying, "I am disgraced. I did not take a palm branch nor did I go to meet the old man, for I am filled with shame, as you yourselves can see." And when the brothers went out and stood before the old man, he greeted them one by one and when he did not see the brother who had been accused of theft, he asked

---

[109]*Pipapa*. Lampe (s.v. *papas*), 1006A, says the word was used as a title of respect for priests and bishops, especially for the bishop of Alexandria, but does not cite monastic usage. Crum, 13B, says *papa* "often in colophons and late documents, with art[icle] *ppapa*, is *papas priest*."

[110]"Thief" in Coptic is *soni*, while "brothers is *snēou* (singular *son*).

[111]That is, to the settled regions of Egypt, either towards Alexandria or the Delta or Babylon (Cairo).

[112]There seems to be a lacuna in the text here.

where he was and the brothers explained to Abba Macarius why the thief was ashamed to come greet him. When Abba Macarius heard this, he laughed and entered the monastery.

The accused brother came humbly to meet him and asked the old man's forgiveness just as Abba Macarius asked forgiveness of the brother, and they accepted forgiveness from each other. Abba Macarius said to the brothers, "Neither I nor you are as honorable as this fellow: not only has he endured [166] great reproach but he has taken upon his head even the sin of the brother who stole the pots." And Abba Macarius restored him to his place. The other brother, however, took up his sheepskin mantle and left that monastery and did not return to it.[113]

Abba Macarius Teaches About What it Takes to Live (AP Macarius 20)

47   Abba Macarius said, "Since reproach has been like honor to you and poverty like wealth or loss like profit or straitened circumstances like wide open spaces or the things of the flesh like strangers, then you will not die but will live. Follow your conscience with your fellows and stay away from anyone who is arrogant."

Abba Macarius Teaches about Desiring the Things of Salvation

48   Abba Macarius the Great said, "I implore you, my brothers, let the things you yearn for be things that lead to salvation and the preservation of your souls so you won't put off something one day for the next and so spend two days as strangers to the good things of God."

[113]Both "restored" and "return" translate Coptic -tasthof.

Abba Macarius Teaches about Vigilance

49   Abba Macarius said, "The way that leads to Gehenna: fasting will lead you there, meditation will lead you there, compassion will lead you there, asceticism will lead you there."

The brothers said to him, "Does humility also lead one there, our father?"

He said, "True humility is not merely [167] saying with the mouth 'Forgive me.' God's way is a heart that has cut itself off from everything that leads it. Furthermore, let us not cause the person who prepares himself in advance to be negligent before the gates of the city center have been shut and no one is able to buy or sell. Nor has it been said, 'Open the door for the foolish young women who are wailing and weeping and knocking on the door' [Mt 25:1–13], which has been closed to them on account of their negligence. Be vigilant, then, with all vigilance, while you are sitting in your cell or while you are surrounded by people."

Concerning Nighttime Responsibilities

50A   He also said, "Let half the night suffice for your worship and rest your body the other half."[114]

On Fasting

50B   He also said, "The regular fast is to fast until the ninth hour[115] and the person who does more than this will receive greater rewards.

[114]This was apparently also the custom of Pachomius' master Palamon; see *The First Greek Life* 60 and *Bohairic Life* 10; *Pachomian Koinonia*, vol. 1, *The Life of Saint Pachomius and His Disciples*, trans. Armand Veilleux (Kalamazoo: Cistercian, 1980), 339, 31. It was also the practice of Isaiah of Scetis *Precept* 55 (PG 103.432) and 32 (PG 103.340).

[115]Roughly 3 p.m.

On Work

51   Our righteous father, Abba Macarius the Great, said, "Truly, all the works that each of us does are written, whether it be a service or, even more, prayer that one performs at any time; or, even more, kneeling; or, even more, a tear; or, even more, fasting; or a good word that someone says to his brother; or a very insignificant work [168] that someone does for God, including manual labor: all these things are written for us each day. By no means, my children, will our Savior rob you of anything. All the labors that each person does will be shown to them [*sic*] at the time they leave the body. Fight, my children. Do not gaze at the multitude eating and drinking and sleeping, who do not repent.[116] Do not say, 'Perhaps those who suffer and those who do not suffer are really equal.' By no means, my children! Strengthen yourselves in the faith of your land, for every harsh labor that we undertake (surely suffering due to one's ascetic eating habits is one example), even an insignificant ascetic practice that one does, will be revealed to us in the age to come. Run, then, my children, to labor and to love your labor; let it be sweet to you with very great humility of heart.

Abba Macarius Interprets a Mysterious Saying He Hears (AP Macarius 24)

52   Abba Macarius the Great, passing through a village one time with some brothers, heard a young boy say to his mother, "My mother, a rich man loves me and cherishes me, but I detest him. A poor man detests me, but I cherish [169] him."

When Saint Abba Macarius heard these words, he was utterly astonished. The brothers said to him, "What is it about these words, my father, that astonishes you so completely like this?"

The old man struck his chest and said, "What a great mystery there is in these words!"

[116]Literally: *eat their hearts*; see Crum, 478B.

They begged him, "Tell us!"

He said to them, "Truly, my children, the Lord is the rich man: he loves us, but we do not want to obey him. Our enemy, the Devil, is the poor man: he detests us, but we love his filthy acts and abominable practices and vain desires and the rest of his pleasures."

Renouncing the Devil

53 Abba Macarius the Great said, "It is fitting for whoever has renounced the world and entered the monastic life to remember what the holy apostle said. He enumerated the branches of evil when he spoke upbraiding those who had fallen, saying, 'By turning off of the path of virtue and by forsaking the grace of the Holy Spirit, they become reprobate, filled with every kind of wickedness and evil and violence, filled with envy and murder and contentiousness,' and all the other things he spoke about in that passage [Rom 1:29]. He repeated words of this sort when he said, [170] 'Those who do things like this deserve to die' [Rom 1:32]. Therefore, I beseech you, my beloved children in the Lord, keep yourselves away from slander and from every thought that estranges us from Christ the King and befriends the Devil and his demons, since the Devil in fact rejoices, my children, over those who fall into his hands. But I have faith that God's protection will protect you from the Devil's snares."

On Remaining Steadfast

54 Abba Macarius the Great said, "It is fitting for the monk sitting in his cell to be self-collected and to keep himself far from all the cares of the world and not allow himself to wander about among the vanities of this age but to have a single aim: placing his thoughts in God alone at all times, remaining steadfast in him on every occasion, without distraction and without allowing anything earthly to trouble his heart, neither fleshly thinking nor concerns about his parents

nor conversing with loved ones nor the consolation of family; rather, he should maintain his mind and all his faculties as though he were standing before God, that he may fulfill [171] the word of the apostle: 'In order that the virgin might remain fully steadfast in the Lord, without any kind of distraction'" [1 Cor 7:34].

The Monk is Like the Angels

55   Abba Macarius also said, "The rank of monk is like that of the angels. Just as the angels stand in the Lord's presence at all times and no earthly thing hinders them from standing in his presence, so too it is with the monk: it is fitting that he should be like the angels his whole life. In doing this he will fulfill the word of our Savior who commands each of us to deny himself and take up his cross and follow him [Mt 10:38//Lk 14:27]. In the same way, act a little violently, my beloved children, in order that you may acquire virtue for yourselves, and virtue alone, for it is written, 'The kingdom of heaven belongs to those who act violently'" [Mt 11:12].

Fervent in the Spirit

56   Abba Macarius the Great said, "It is fitting that the monk be purified from every passion of the flesh and every stain and that he not allow his thoughts to commingle with evil thoughts at all; instead, he should be fervent in the Spirit at all times" [Rom 12:11].

Making Oneself a Stranger (to God)

57   Abba Macarius also said, "The monk who causes anger makes himself a stranger; [172] the monk who causes his brother pain in anything makes himself a stranger."

Abba Macarius Warns about Coming Evil Times[117]

58   Abba Macarius the Great said, "A time is coming when numerous sufferings will come to those who keep monastic practices; as a result, they will forget renunciation and abstinence, and the powerful king of that time will oppress them."

The brothers said to him, "What sort of king will he be?"

Abba Macarius said to them, "He will be half-Ishmaelite; the generations of his loins come from Esau. *Our* King is our Lord Jesus Christ; furthermore, his offspring are virtue and purity and purity and cleanliness of soul and body. The earthly king's power comes from our king, the king of heaven, Christ the true God. But the earthly king is a lover of gold, he is a lover of silver and a lover of pleasure; like stallions mad for mares, he is a lover of luxury, worshipping women and horses like gods. He is a lover of the passions in everything he does; he searches out and puts his faith in earthly things, thinking that he will also possess them in the life to come on account of the many pleasures that they bring him, and he expends all his efforts in gaining possession [173] of the whole earth and boasting about it, tyrannizing the earth's inhabitants; he will shackle the earth with iron chains ‹and›[118] numerous sufferings and scores of prisons, and without Christ the King."

The brothers said to him, "What will become of the fathers of that time?"

Abba Macarius said to them, "They will be tightly shackled so that some will despair and will forget the angelic life on account of love of money. Our Lord Jesus Christ will be patient with them when

[117]This saying appears to contain references to Islam or the Arabs which, if taken as prophecy *ex eventu*, would place its composition after the Arab invasion of Egypt in 641. "Ishmaelites" in the Old Testament refers to nomads living in the desert regions of North Arabia. Ishmael was the son of Abraham by his maidservant Hagar (Gen 25:18–19); Arabs trace their ancestry to Ishmael (Ismail) rather than Isaac, the other son of Abraham. Esau was traditionally seen as the ancestor of the Edomites (Gen 36, Mal 1:2–3).

[118]Reading *mbenipi nem* instead of *mbenipi nkhen*, which also fits with the rest of the sentence.

SAINT MACARIUS THE SPIRITBEARER

he sees the choice they have made. They will reveal their true nature by gathering together the things they have made with their hands and buyers and sellers will multiply among them as they do among the worldly. Under the pretext of performing public acts, they will seek out the things of the flesh and will forget passionlessness. Whoever you find among the fathers of that time who keeps himself pure from eating and drinking to excess on account of numerous laxities and who protects his body from the world's sexual sins and the love of money and who does not judge those brothers who fall will be blessed in the presence of Christ, the King of Glory, and will be accounted an offspring of the promise and an inheritor of life eternal [174] and will appear before Christ the King with great confidence."[119]

Vigilance During Prayer

59 Abba Macarius said, "It is fitting for the monk, as the body allows, to not cry out during prayers nor abandon his practice of prayer because of a single prostration, but rather while he prays to pay attention for an opening of his spirit, anticipating when God will come and visit the soul's exits and spiritual organs[120] and all its pathways. Thus, if the hour comes, whether we be silent or cry out in prayer, let the spirit be vigilant, contemplating the Lord at all times."[121]

[119]The sentence beginning with "Whoever" begins with a singular subject but switches to the plural with "will be accounted" to the end of the sentence, probably under the influence of the pseudo-passive plural verb (*senaer han makarios*).

[120]*Aisthēterion*; see Lampe 53B(3).

[121]A slightly longer version of this saying may be found as *Homily* 33.1 by Pseudo-Macarius; see *Pseudo-Macarius: The Fifty Spiritual Homilies and The Great Letter*, trans. George A. Maloney (Classics of Western Spirituality; New York: Paulist, 1992), 201.

A Warning to the Soul

60 Abba Macarius again said, "Woe to the soul that has not implored and entreated the Lord to rest in it and purify it from every blemish and every stain and keep it free from wild beasts and reptiles, which are the spirits of evil that take the form of small creatures and gnats that fly in the night: if they see a light at a distance or a burning wick, they come to it and fly into the flame and burn up in it. [175] So it is with the monk who impels himself in all things by his own choice and free will: he will be found in the eternal fire."

The Soul that Bears Spiritual Fruit

61 Abba Macarius again said, "Like Aaron's staff, which brought forth flowers in a single night and bore fruit [Num 17, Heb 9:4], thus it is with the soul of the monk: when the Lord comes to it, it puts forth spiritual flowers by means of the things that belong to Christ and bears the fruits of the Spirit and gives them to him who created it, Christ, its good King, the true and blessed God."

God's Gifts to the Penitent

62 Abba Macarius the Great said, "If someone undertakes to know and search out God and if he repents the things he has done during his periods of negligence, God gives him a heart troubled about the things he has done.[122] Afterwards, through his compassion, God graces him with bodily suffering by means of fastings and prayers and numerous vigils and renunciation of matter and self-contempt and hatred of bodily comfort and love of tears more than laughter and renunciation of his family according to the flesh."[123]

[122]The troubled heart is a gift of repentance, which here in Coptic is literally "to eat the heart."

[123]See #5 above.

Abba Macarius Learns about True Work

63 [176] It was said about Abba Macarius the Great that, passing through Egypt one time, he came upon a threshing floor. He saw a heap of grain that had been threshed, its owner using it to pay wages to the workers. When the old man wished to test the grower, wishing him to talk about the nature of his work, he said to him, "Please do me the kindness, my father, of giving me a little wheat."

The grower said to him, "If you have worked, I will pay you a wage, for whoever works receives a wage."

The old man said to him, "You're right. Whoever works receives a wage."

The grower said to him, "Yes, just like I said: whoever works receives a wage."

The old man said to him, "This is just what I wanted to hear from you."

When he was some distance away on his journey, Abba Macarius slapped himself in the face with his hands and said, "Woe to you, Macarius! They have refused to give you a wage for the fleshly work of this world, since it is written, 'Hasten to use the worker who has not been ashamed to do his master's work well' [2 Tim 2:15]. Woe to you, then, Macarius! You have failed to obtain that goodness of the master of the vineyard who says, 'Call the workers, give them [177] their wage, the last, the first, a measure to each' [Mt 20:1–16], and 'Whoever works, his wage is not reckoned to him a gift' " [Rom 4:4]. And so the old man Macarius continued walking, mourning with tears and groaning.

More Concerning Repentance

64 Abba Macarius said, "Like the carpenter who straightens what is crooked and bends what is straight, so it is with the repentance that our Lord Jesus Christ has appointed for us: it makes what is

crooked and rolls in the filth of sin straight again and makes it pure
like virgins standing in the presence of our Lord Jesus Christ. Those
who turn away from their sins and repent receive the pure angelic
habit that is in heaven."

Advice for Teachers and Monastic Leaders

65 Abba Macarius the Great said, "If fingerprint marks from the
hand of the teacher and the head of the monastery[124] are not found
carved on the cheek of the person[125] who places himself in submission to them with great patience and without murmuring, it is not
possible for this person to receive the crown and the wage of perfect
sonship nor the honor of the disciples of our Lord Jesus Christ, [178]
for the teacher has received the likeness and the form of the true
shepherd, the true teacher, he who allowed the strokes of nails and
the stroke of the lance to be carved in his body as a testimony and a
reproval against the Jews; and these things he accepted voluntarily
with great gentleness. In the same way, if those who are harbors and
superiors of those who place themselves in submission to them do
not possess goodness[126] and sweetness, it is not possible for them to
beget spiritual sons like Elijah, who begot Elisha, and like Paul, who
begot Timothy and Onesimus [1 Kg 19:16–21, 2 Kg 2:19–22, Acts
16–20, 1 Thess 1:1, Philem 1:10].

Abba Paphnutius Tells about Abba Macarius and the Ferryman

66 Abba Paphnutius,[127] the true disciple of Abba Macarius, spoke:
"It was once revealed to the old man concerning a ferryman who had

[124]*Koinobioarchēs*; see John Moschus *Pratum spirituale* 97.
[125]I take this to mean slap marks.
[126]Accepting Am's reading of *oumetchrēstos* for *metchr̄s*.
[127]See #74 below. In *AP* Macarius 28 and 37 Paphnutius is described as "the dis-

a virtue but, on account of the veil of darkness spread over his heart and the despondency that gripped him each day, did not know or understand it. The old man rose and went to the Nile and saw the ferryman, who possessed no understanding of God. Abba Macarius was astonished when he saw the ferryman's lack of fear[128] [179] and stopped and reflected on the man's wretched condition. When the day ended, the ferryman went home. 'I myself,' Macarius said, 'followed him and when I met his wife and we sat down, I saw what had been revealed to me earlier but saw none of the things that God had revealed to me except for seven children who entered the house. Afterwards I asked the ferryman about the virtue and his work, and he said to me, "The virtue is dung,"[129] because God had hidden the work from him for his own good. When I saw his lack of understanding, I entreated God to open his heart, and the Lord heard me right away and opened the man's understanding and knowledge and he became fearful and was groaning and his tears flowed to the ground. I was astonished at the consolation[130] that he now had. He said to me, "Now God has opened my heart and what I have learned has enabled me to understand the things inside me all the time, the things that God had caused me to forget for the good of my soul and body: When God joined me to my wife according to the ways of the world and I was still sleeping with her, my wife and I agreed on a covenant between ourselves, with God and with one another, to safe-

ciple of Abba Macarius"; in the *Life of Macarius of Scetis* 36 he is described as "the holy man Abba Paphnutius, who was the greatest of the saint's disciples. It was he who assumed the fatherhood in the holy places after Abba Macarius." Cassian uses Paphnutius as a spokesman for *Conferences* 3. He was also the leader of Scetis, or at least one of its "congregations," when Cassian was there; see the story in *Conferences* 10.2 (on the Anthropomorphites). See also the discussion in Columba Stewart, *Cassian the Monk* (New York: Oxford, 1998), 10–11; Tim Vivian, *Paphnutius: Histories of the Monks of Upper Egypt and the Life of Onnophrius* (Kalamazoo: Cistercian, 1993; rev. ed., 2000), 42–50; and Jean-Claude Guy, *Les Apophtegmes des Pères: Collection Systématique, Chapitres I-IX* (SC 387; Paris: Cerf, 1993), 59–61.

[128]Lacking the fear of God; see below.

[129]Taking *hōs* to equal *hos*, "dung." Am translates "un chant," accepting the reading as *hōs*, "song, hymn," but this makes no sense.

[130]-*paraklēsis*.

guard our purity until we left [179] this world. And since then I have not known what it is like to sleep with my wife, nor she with me, nor do I know whose these children are or how she bore them, and, through the grace of God, I have not said a word of reproach to her. Look! I accept frost and scorching heat supporting these eight souls, being ignorant of the grace that our Lord Jesus Christ has worked for me." When he finished saying these things to me, I threw myself on his neck and kissed him. I left him, giving glory to our Lord Jesus Christ for the numerous graces that he has worked for human beings for the salvation of their souls in order that through every opportunity we may obtain the eternal life of the kingdom of heaven through the many acts of compassion that he does for us.' "

Abba Macarius Teaches about Attending to the Lord in Prayer

67 Abba Macarius the Great said, "If you pursue prayer, pay careful attention to yourself lest you place your pots in the hands of your enemies, for they desire to steal your pots, which are the thoughts of your soul. These are the precious pots with which you will serve God, for God does not look for you to glorify him only with your lips, while your thoughts wander to and fro and [181] are scattered throughout the world, but requires that your soul and all its thoughts wait upon the sight of the Lord without distraction, for he is the great physician, the healer of souls and bodies, our Lord Jesus Christ. Let us beseech him to heal the illnesses of our souls and illumine our thoughts and the perceptions of our hearts that we may understand his great love for humanity and the suffering that he undertook in the world for us and the good things he has done for us day after day, although we are unworthy, for he is our master and savior, our Lord Jesus Christ."

Teachings about the Anchoritic Life[131]

68   A brother asked Abba Macarius about withdrawal. The old man said to him, "If you want to live the anchoritic life,[132] patiently endure it with all forbearance and do not spend one day inside and one day outside but patiently endure it and God and his grace will dwell with you. Do not concern yourself with the shameful thoughts of others nor allow any pretext to take away a day from you unless it affords an opportunity to assist your poor brother or whoever is [182] in need or is suffering. But if God determines that his need will be met through someone else or through his brothers, go home and patiently endure your poverty so that the sweetness of solitude may continuously be with you.

"Do not loiter outside lest the scorching heat rise up against you and all your work be in vain and you weary yourself over and over until you use up all your water. No, remain in your dwelling; patiently endure your poverty and consolation will come to you along with the joy and gladness of the Savior.

"Do not have friendships with anyone except your brothers in poverty.[133] Do not run to anyone on account of some good that he has done for you; run to God alone. Serve him; it is he who serves you in the compassion of sonship. Stay away from friendships with people; keep all your friendship between yourself and God. Do not run to anyone to relax with him in friendship nor converse freely with him in his home nor visit with him in obedience to any commandment lest you be a bother.

"My brother, if you wish to be at peace your whole life, let your thoughts be united with God at all times. Keep yourself from friendship with people. [183] If your brother according to the flesh comes to see you and you do not wish to reject him, take him, give him to

[131]For sayings in a similar vein, see Tim Vivian and Birger A. Pearson, "Saint Paul of Tamma on the Monastic Cell (de Cella)," *Hallel*, 23:2 (1998), 86–107.

[132]*-anachōritēs*; "withdrawal" immediately above translates *-anachōrisis*.

[133]On poverty as both monastic ideal and self-designation, see Vivian and Pearson, "Saint Paul of Tamma," 92.

another brother whom the brothers trust because he is faithful. You stay poor; do not lose the rich treasure [awaiting you].[134]

"Four men were heads of four works in the Old Testament.[135] The first was Abraham, whose door was open to everyone and who was a servant to every image of God.[136] He stood serving strangers and washed the feet of the Lord and his angels [Gen 18:1–5], for God gave him his free will when he appeared to him; he established with him his covenant and his work has been shown to be the head of the Church, bringing souls to God [Gen 18]. Moses guided the people in the desert while God spoke with him face to face; he too was the head of his work [Ex 14–15, 33–34]. Lazarus, although ill, gave thanks for his illness, and was patient in his suffering and distress, watching the rich of this age eat and drink the good things of this life in his presence; they did not have pity[137] on him for a single day but he nevertheless gave thanks in his simple sincerity and [184] guilelessness and without complaint. Our Lord bore witness concerning him that he was perfect in his work and head of it [Lk 16:19–31]. Elijah in his poverty lived in the desert without cares and concerns, and God served him. He too was head of his work [1 Kings 17].

"Now then, my brother, since you too desire to live well in renunciation and poverty as someone poor and humble who casts his cares and concerns on God, bound to his dwelling, patiently enduring his poverty, and also purifying his thoughts toward every image of God, I will not be able to speak about its honor: the Lord is the one who knows the honor of this virtue; but mercy belongs to our Lord Jesus Christ who, out of his great compassion, will honor us."

[134]Am suggests that some text is lost here.

[135]The four works seem to be hospitality (Abraham), openness to God (Moses), patient endurance (Lazarus), and poverty (Elijah), although Lazarus is misplaced.

[136]That is, to human beings and angels.

[137]"Have pity" translates *-shen hēt*, while "patient" is *-ōou hēt* (*hēt* is Coptic for "heart").

Abba Macarius Explains the Value of Remaining in One's Cell

69 It was said concerning Abba Macarius that a brother came to see him one time and told him, "My father, my thoughts say to me, 'Go, visit the sick,' for this, it is said, is a great commandment."

Abba Macarius said to him a prophetic word: "It was the mouth without lie, our Lord Jesus Christ, who said, 'I was sick and you visited me' [Mt 25:36].[138] He took on human flesh and made it one with himself and he took on humanity in everything except sin [185] alone [Heb 4:15], but I say to you, my child, sitting in your cell is better for you than visiting, for afterwards a time will come when they will mock those who remain in their cells and the word of Abba Antony will be fulfilled: 'If they see someone who is not mad, they will rise up against him and say, "You are mad!" because he is not like them.'[139] I say to you, my child, if Moses had not entered the darkness, he would not have been given the tablets of the covenant written by the finger of God [Ex 19–23].[140]

Abba Pambo Recounts a Visit to Abba Macarius

70 Abba Pambo said,[141] "In my heart I decided to kiss the hands of Abba Macarius the Spiritbearer[142] one more time while I was still in

[138]Visiting the sick had perhaps a linguistic relationship for the monks: "sick" is *shōni*, while "visit" is *-shini*.

[139]*AP* Antony 25 (Ward, 6).

[140]Am then prints *eouōou* and notes, 185 n. 2, that the formula that concludes this sentence is the beginning of the doxologies found at the end of Coptic works (see #82 below). "One could conclude," he says, "that the work ends here and that the remainder is an addition. But I do not believe that this is the case. In the margin one reads, 'Start the fourth (reading). Begin. Appoint this (passage) to be read on the fourth Saturday. Say the preceding passage on the fourth Sunday.'" Am's statement, however, is based on a misreading of the text; the text reads *ejōou*.

[141]In *AP* Macarius 2, Pambo (*Pamō* in Coptic) appears to be a priest at Nitria whom Macarius goes to visit.

[142]On "Spiritbearer" see the Introduction to this volume; see #82 below.

the body. When I went south to the ravine[143] of Abba Moses, I came upon Abba Poemen and Abba Evagrius the Wise and Abba Chronius and two other brothers who were with us at Abba Moses'. I had come with a number of thoughts but I found just one sticking with me. After the sun had set, [186] there came thunder and lightning and stormy darkness and very strong tornado-like winds. We were at a loss as to how we would enjoy and obtain the blessing of the holy Spiritbearer Abba Macarius the Great. One of us said, 'The comforting Holy Spirit that dwells in Abba Macarius will show us a sign and will guide us in peace to Abba Macarius.'

"The seven of us left. We stood and prayed. And there was an adze[144] on the lintel of the rock of Abba Macarius and suddenly we saw a column of fire: it stood over the lintel, flaming and shining brightly, rising high up to heaven, and while we were still walking, the column descended with us little by little into the ravine. When we came to the rock of Saint Abba Macarius, the column descended and we saw the inside of his dwelling glowing like fire. We knocked at the door and the saint came out. When we saw the light shining on his face, we fell to the ground and prostrated ourselves at his holy feet. He raised us up and greeted each of us [187] with a kiss. After we prayed, we sat and spoke of the glory that comes with making progress in God, along with the good way of life and the establishment of monastic practice in Scetis. Afterwards Abba Macarius replied and said, 'My brothers, one of you seven will be perfected in battle as a martyr and seven other brothers will also be perfected with him in the same way.'

"Abba Moses replied, 'Remember me, my father, that the word of the Savior may be fulfilled for me, "Everyone who takes up the sword will die by the sword" [Mt 26:52].[145] This indeed is the hope that I look forward to.'

---

[143]-*janē*; see Crum, 819B, who cites Gk *koilos* and *egkoilos* ("hollow, ravine") as Greek equivalents.

[144]*Skeplari*; Am: *pic*. It is clear from M.Gr. *skeparni* that this is the more correctly spelled *skepari* from ancient *skeparnon*.

[145]Moses the Black had been a thief and murderer before his conversion. He died

"After these words we threw ourselves down and received a blessing from him and the holy old man prayed over us. He dismissed us and we walked, giving glory to God for the conversation that we had had and for the sight we had seen,[146] and we too were zealous for the great graces that God does for his saints."

Abba Macarius Teaches a Brother about Forgiveness

71   A brother fell on account of a transgression and went to Abba Macarius in tears, saying, "Pray[147] for me, my father, because I have fallen into the sickness of Sodom; I have stumbled doing that which you already know about."

[188] Abba Macarius said to him, "Have courage, my child. Take hold of that which is outside of time, that which is without beginning, that which will endure forever, which has no end, the help of those who have no hope except in him alone, the sweet name on every person's lips, the sole sweetness, the perfect life, who possesses numerous treasuries of compassion, our Lord Jesus Christ, our true God. May he be your consolation and helper and the one who forgives you. My child, I say to you, if a virgin falls on account of a transgression and preserves herself as she was originally created,[148] I say to you that if she is joyful on account of the shame on her face and the scorn heaped on her, Christ rejoices over her as though over a virgin. It is the same with you, my child, since you have revealed your shame, as Holy Scripture says, 'Confess your sins to one another so that entreaty may be made for you and you may be forgiven and be saved' [Jas 5:16], for Peter said to the Lord, 'How many times shall I forgive my brother? Up to seven times?' The good God said to him,

in the first barbarian raid on Scetis in 407–8, along with seven companions; see AP Moses 10, where Moses also refers to the saying from Matthew.

[146]That is, of the pillar.

[147]Or: intercede; *tōbh.*

[148]*Plasma* is the human person as created by God, part of the *plasis.* Thus, of her "created body," virginity is a part—a detachable one.

'I do not say to you seven times but seven times seventy times'" [Mt 18:21].

Abba Macarius Compares a Monk to a Person Who Takes a Bath

72 Abba Macarius said, "If someone goes [189] to the baths and does not strip off all his clothes, he is not able to bathe nor wash off all his filth; so it is with someone who makes progress as a monk: if he does not strip off all concerns of this world with all its desires filled with vain pleasures, he is not able to advance or make progress in virtue nor be victorious over all the arrows of the Enemy, which are filth."

Abba Macarius Compares the Spiritual Father to the Pilot of a Ship

73 Abba Macarius the Great said, "The pilot of a ship, that is, the steersman, risks danger with the ship and the cargo until he brings his ship into port; so is it with a spiritual father who has children with him and is concerned for their safety. For the ship's pilot is never without concern for his ship but examines his fastenings, to see which of them is leaking water or which is bad until he seals all of them lest he sink in the waters and perish. So too is it with the father who has authority over the brothers: it is necessary for him to examine all the passions and [190] pleasures and evil thoughts of the demons that the brothers have to see how all these passions are leaking evil water in their souls, lest he show a lack of concern about the opportunities of the flesh and be in danger and be accused before God because he forgot the training of the brothers who were with him until they were shipwrecked and drowned in the sea and the tyrannical waves of the insidious demons, the enemy of renunciation and abstinence."

Abba Macarius' Many Saving Virtues (AP Macarius 32; Sayings 22)

74   It was said about Abba Macarius the Great that a cherub[149] remained by him from the day that he began to make progress, strengthening his resolve and fortifying him for abstinence, and in these things he made progress daily, advancing in the sweetness of virtue so that his good fame spread throughout the entire Roman Empire and the East, for he attracted everyone to himself and brought them into the angelic practice on account of the sweet incense of his exalted ascetic practices; as a result, he snatched a multitude from the mouth of death for life eternal. Our Lord Jesus Christ gave him the grace to see people's sins [191] like oil placed in a glass jar and he would cover all of them, being like God.[150]

Abba Paphnutius Tells about a Godly Worker

75   Abba Paphnutius, the true disciple of Abba Macarius, said, "It was revealed to the old man that a certain worker worked without murmuring and possessed great patience, placing his hope in the reward[151] of eternal life. He got up hurriedly and said to me, 'Get up. Follow me.' We walked and came to a secluded spot of the Nile and while we were sitting in silence, the old man was held rapt by a vision. I spoke to him with frankness since I was on firm ground with him and knew that through the grace of our Lord Jesus Christ nothing was impossible with him, 'My father, do you not command me to say what is on my mind?'

     "He said to me, 'My child, what is it?'

---

[149]Text: cherubim; see #1. This cherub is an important presence in the *Life of Macarius of Scetis*.

[150]The image of oil and water is clear, but the use of "cover" with it muddies the metaphor a bit. However, because this last clause is also found in *AP Macarius* 32 (Ward, 134) // Coptic *Sayings* 22, I have translated the sentence literally; see Coptic *Sayings* 22 above and the note there.

[151]*Becke* also means "wages"; see below.

"I replied to him, 'Fashion a prayer so we may cross the river.'

"He responded and spoke to me with a face filled with joy and a mouth filled with grace, 'My child, will we emulate our Lord Jesus Christ or acquire the strength of Peter, the leader of the apostles [Mt 14:29], or will we be able to flee from human vainglory even when people heap praises on us?'

"When he finished saying these things, [192] a beast that lives in the waters suddenly appeared! Saint Abba Macarius said to it, 'Is it the wish of our Lord Jesus Christ that you cross the river, or not?' As soon as he said this, the beast came to shore and when we had climbed on top of it, it took us to the opposite side. When we lept ashore, my father Abba Macarius said to it, 'Use force. Plunge your head under water and our Lord Jesus Christ will give you your fare.'[152] It plunged under water and immediately appeared with a great fish! When I saw this great wonder, I threw myself down at his feet, being very fearful, but he raised me up. Thus we walked, giving glory to our Lord Jesus Christ.

"When we drew near to the village we sat down and our righteous father Abba Macarius observed those who were passing by. Suddenly he saw the worker coming, clothed with the grace of patience. He said, 'Behold, a chosen and precious vessel' [Acts 9:15]! He got up and greeted the worker with a kiss and said to him, 'Peace be with you, worker of the eleventh hour.'[153]

"He in turn replied, 'According to the will of my Lord Jesus Christ.'

"Our father Abba Macarius said to him, 'What kind of work do you do [193] and who pays you your wages?'

"The worker said to him, 'I work for a landowner, and the king in heaven pays me my wages.'

"My father Abba Macarius said to him, 'Are you sure this is the case?'

[152]For a similar story concerning a crocodile, but one with quite a different ending, see *Historia Monachorum* XII.6–7 (Abba Helle); Russell, 90–91.

[153]See the parable in Mt 20:1–16, which figures further in the conversation between Macarius and the worker.

"The worker said to him, 'I am sure about what the master of the vineyard said.'[154]

"My father Abba Macarius said to him, 'What can you say about this?'

"The worker said to him, 'He said, "Call the workers and pay them their wages." '

"When he finished saying these things, we knelt and prayed then got up and walked. Our father Abba Macarius was grieving and said, 'Woe to you, Macarius! Unlike this secular worker, I am not sure that my work is pleasing to my Lord Jesus Christ or that I am at all worthy of an earthly wage, much less a heavenly one.'

"Afterwards, when we came to the Nile, my holy father Abba Macarius said to me, 'My child, let us too travel like others do.' We boarded the ferry and put to the west, and when we had traveled ahead a little, my father Abba Macarius said to me, 'Let us sit awhile, my child,' and while we were sitting as though in a trance, [194] I was not aware of anything until we found ourselves beside the cave. I said to him, 'We got here quickly, my father.'

"He said to me, 'Let us give glory to our Lord Jesus Christ, for it was he who seized Habakkuk and Philip [Bel 1:33–36, Acts 8:39]. It was also he who guided us.' "

Abba Macarius Heals a Serpent through the Compassion of Christ

76 Abba Macarius said, "While we were still sitting in the cave one time, I heard a voice crying out like the voice of a falcon, and when I went outside I saw a huge serpent. When it saw me, it bent its neck and venerated me and afterwards it raised itself and turned its face toward me. When I looked at it, I saw that there was something[155] lodged in his right eye. When I thought about the compassion of my

---

[154]The abbreviation for "master" used in the text also means "Lord," that is, Christ.

[155]*Joul*, meaning uncertain. Crum, 765B, cites only this passage and suggests "fragment," while Am translates "une paille," a piece of straw.

Lord Jesus Christ and the invincible power of the cross, I put some spittle on the serpent's face while saying, 'My Lord Jesus Christ, who opened the eyes of the man born blind, have pity on this beast's infirmity and heal it' [Jn 9]. When I said this, the fragment fell from its eye and after it bent its neck three times it kissed my feet and so I dismissed it. It left, giving glory to our Lord Jesus Christ for his numerous acts of compassion, for he even cares about wild beasts."

Abba Macarius Teaches Abba Evagrius about Evil Thoughts

77 [195] Abba Evagrius asked Abba Macarius while he was sitting beside him with some other brothers, "How does Satan find all these evil thoughts to throw at the brothers?"

Abba Macarius said to him, "Whoever kindles a fire in an oven holds a lot of kindling in his hands and does not hesitate to throw it into the fire. So too the Devil: he kindles fires and does not hesitate to throw into everyone's heart all kinds of evil kindling, that is, defilements. We see moreover that water extinguishes and is victorious over the power of the fire. So it is with the help of the Protector, our Lord Jesus Christ, and the invincible power of the cross: if we throw our weaknesses at his feet, all of Satan's evil branches are extinguished in us and our Lord Jesus Christ causes our hearts to burn and boil in the Spirit with celestial fire and be filled with rejoicing."[156]

Abba Macarius Teaches Abba Evagrius about Patience and Self-Denial[157]

78 Abba Evagrius also said, "I paid a visit to Abba Macarius at the hottest time of the day. I was burning with thirst and said to him, 'I am very thirsty, my father.'

[156]See *AP* Macarius the Great 12 (Ward, 130) for a similar (though not, apparently, parallel) saying.

[157]This saying is found in essentially the same form in Evagrius *Praktikos* 94; see

"He said to me, 'Let the shade suffice. There are numbers of people [196] on the road right now who are burning who have no shade.'

"After these words I talked with him about virtue. He said to me, 'Truly, my child, I have spent twenty years without filling my heart with bread or water or sleep, although I have reclined against the wall until I snatched a little sleep.' "[158]

Listening to the Word of God

79   Abba Macarius the Great said, "Knowing as you do that you rejoice in the voice of the Lord, listen to it not only to listen but in order to learn to obey it, for whoever listens to the word of God with

A. and C. Guillaumont, *Évagre le Pontique: Traité pratique ou le moine* (SC 170–71; Paris: Cerf, 1971), 171:698 and, for an English translation, *Evagrius Ponticus: The Praktikos and Chapters on Prayer*, trans. John Eudes Bamberger (Kalamazoo: Cistercian, 1981), 40. Antoine Guillaumont believes, however, that the "holy father Macarius" referred to in *Praktikos* 94 is not Macarius of Egypt but Macarius of Alexandria, despite the clear reference in *Praktikos* 93 to Macarius the Egyptian. See his "Le problème des deux Macaires," esp. 51–52 (Guillaumont does not refer to the *Virtues*). He believes that Evagrius "generally designated" Macarius of Alexandria with the epithet "the holy father Macarius." In the *Life of Macarius of Alexandria* 12 the saying is attributed to the Alexandrian. In *Virtues* 74 (Amélineau, 193), Paphnutius refers to Macarius of Egypt as "my holy father Abba Macarius" (*paiōt ethouab abba makarios*), but in support of Guillaumont, in the *Virtues* Evagrius always refers to Macarius simply as "Abba Macarius." Furthermore, it is more likely that Evagrius would drop by and visit Macarius the Alexandrian at mid-day since they both lived in the Cells. When Evagrius visited Macarius the Egyptian, he had to make the perilous journey from Kellia to Scetis; it is hard to believe that Macarius would deny Evagrius water after such a journey. Macarius the Alexandrian was noteworthy for the extremes of his fasting. The Macarii were often confused in antiquity, even though the two were quite different in personality. The *Apophthegmata* confuses the two to some degree and the *Historia monachorum* thoroughly confuses them (though interestingly, Rufinus' Latin translation of the *Historia monachorum* corrects the Greek version, probably because Rufinus had actually met Macarius the Alexandrian). Socrates and Sozomen are also somewhat confused. Only eyewitnesses—like Evagrius and Rufinus—seem to get it right. It is therefore not surprising that the *Virtues* does make such an occasional and, in this case, very understandable error. For further details, see Guillaumont.

[158]See *Life of Macarius of Alexandria* 12 (in the companion volume to this one, *Four Desert Fathers*).

all his ability learns to obey it. A multitude have heard the word of God but have not heard it with the power of God and with gladness; therefore they have not made progress. Our Lord Jesus Christ speaks about people like this, crying out, 'Whoever has ears to hear, let him hear' [Mt 11:15; 13:9, 43]. If they had not all stopped listening, he would not have spoken like this: 'Whoever has ears to hear, let him hear.' For our Lord Jesus Christ knows that the nature of the Devil is to fight against souls in order to stop them from hearing the word of God and be saved. Therefore he said, 'Whoever has ears to hear, [197] let him hear,' since those who listen make progress and are victorious over all the passions of the soul and the body.

"But if the Devil stops the soul from hearing the word of God with power, she does not advance nor finds a way to fight against the passions of the body because the word of God does not reside in her. If the Enemy uses force against her, she does not find the means to cast away from her any of the evil passions at all, but the soul that possesses the word is good at chasing the passions away from herself and casts out Satan, who flees from her, covered with shame, for so it is written in the apostle: 'The word of God pierces[159] more than any two-edged sword and will enter into the divisions of the soul and the joints and the marrow' [Heb 4:12].[160]

"We can see how if a person is allowed to hear the word of God, he drives away the passions, but if he is not allowed to hear, the soul becomes like lead, driving away none of the evil thoughts. Therefore the Devil despises people like this; even if people like this have spent their whole life in monasticism and virginity, they have progressed in nothing; moreover they have not known [198] the sweetness of God, which is sweeter than honey and the honeycomb [Ps 19:10]; moreover, they have not known the power of God, which is more powerful than anything and strengthens and empowers and encourages the soul day after day, for it is written, 'The heart of the right-

---

[159]"Pierces" translates *hioui* while "casts out" renders *hioui ebol.*
[160]See Heb 4:12: "The word of God is sharper than any two-edged sword, piercing until it divides soul from spirit, joints from marrow."

eous person is more courageous than that of a lion' [2 Sam 17:10].

"Do you see, my children, how the heart of the righteous person is courageous? Why is it courageous? Because it allows him to receive spiritual nourishment, that is, the word of God. For this reason his soul is courageous, like a person who allows himself to take bodily nourishment because it gives him strength from day to day. Therefore, if he does not allow himself to eat and take nourishment, his body loses strength. If his enemies fight him, they will quickly defeat him. Now, then, my beloved, train yourselves also to eat food like this, which is the word of God, in order to be victorious over your enemies, for there are large numbers of monks and virgins who have lived their whole lives without the demons allowing them to eat spiritual food so they might find the strength and courage to defeat their enemies. Why have some not allowed themselves to eat? Because their heart is not straight nor do they resist the heart's desires because their heart is defiled and they lack the least knowledge of God. On account of this, the demons do not allow them to take holy nourishment so they may strengthen their souls. For this reason, they have spent their whole lives [199] in cowardice and stupefaction and affliction, blaming themselves and one another their whole life. Protect yourselves, therefore, from this evil fruit, my beloved, that you may live and be counted partakers of God in Christ Jesus our Savior."

The Parable of the Sheepfold

80 Abba Macarius the Great said, "One time when I was passing through Egypt I came upon a sheepfold with some sheep in it. I saw a sheep outside the sheepfold that had given birth and a wolf came and snatched her offspring and she was weeping, saying, 'Woe is me! If I had not been outside the sheepfold, the wolf would not have found me and snatched my lamb!'"

While he was marveling at what the sheep had said, the brothers who were traveling with him asked him the meaning of what the sheep had said. He responded, saying, "There will come a time when the monks will abandon the deserts where they live and will gather together and become a numerous people. If someone gets separated from them, the spiritual wolf will snatch that person's offspring, that is, his spirit, and he will become more unfeeling than the stones and irrational things, like animals that have no reason. Whichever of the brothers looks for him pridefully and without consulting others will not find him, even though he is right in their midst."

The Lord Answers the Cry of Abba Macarius (AP Macarius 14)

81   [200] It was said about Abba Macarius that one time as he was going up from Scetis to Egypt he was carrying some baskets.[161] When he grew weary, he sat down. He raised his eyes up to heaven and said, "Lord, it is you who see my weariness," and after he said this, he found himself at the Nile with the baskets.

Abba Macarius Teaches Evagrius about Blaspheming against the Holy Spirit

82   Abba Evagrius said, "I was sitting one time with some brothers beside Abba Macarius. He was speaking to us about the sense of the Holy Scriptures and I asked the old man, 'What does this saying in the Gospels mean: "Whoever blasphemes against the Holy Spirit will not be forgiven, either in this age or in the age to come"' [Mt 12:31–32; Mk 3:29//Lk 12:10].

"The old man said to me, 'It is clear that if a person does not possess strong hope and firm faith every time he has a sinful desire, as the Lord said in the Gospel, "If you have faith like a mustard seed,

---

[161]Macarius would have been traveling east (or north- or southeast) from Scetis, toward the Nile, hence to "Egypt," that is, toward Alexandria or Babylon (Cairo), hence non-desert.

you will say to this mountain, 'Move from there,' and it will move and nothing will be impossible for you" [Mt 17:20//Lk 17:6], but rather sins from his earliest days up to the end of his life and says in his heart, "If I return to God, there is no way he will forgive me or accept me," then this person has blasphemed against the power of the Holy Trinity and has allowed Satan inside himself and a sin like this is unforgivable: he has not turned to God and repented with his whole heart. Again, it is like someone who has a physical malady: if he does not have faith in help from on high like Job and the paralytic [Job 42, Mt 9:2], truly such a person blasphemes against the power of the Holy Trinity and, even worse, has allowed Satan inside himself, and sin like this is unforgivable: his sentence is to be cast eternally into Tartarus and the outer darkness where there will be weeping and gnashing of teeth [Mt 8:12]. But the repentance of all these persons is mere spittle spat in the presence of the mercy and compassion of him who possesses treasuries of compassion, our Lord Jesus Christ.'

"When Saint Abba Macarius the Righteous finished saying these things, great courage filled us and spiritual rejoicing. It was as though we had seen Christ the King standing in our midst encouraging us. After all these words that he spoke to us filled with life and healing for our souls from the mouth of the Paraclete who dwelt in Abba Macarius the Great, [202] we threw ourselves on our faces and venerated his holy feet and he prayed over us. We left him, giving thanks and glorifying our Lord Jesus Christ."

Abba Macarius the Spiritbearer

83   Abba Poemen said, "Every time I met Abba Macarius I did not say a single word without his already having knowledge of it because he was a Spiritbearer and possessed a prophetic spirit, like Elijah and all the other prophets, for he was clothed with humility like a cloak through the power of the Paraclete who dwelt in him. He alone pos-

sessed foresight and was filled with the grace of God; the glory of the Lord shone on his face; the consolation of the Consoler, the Holy Spirit, which was with him, came down upon everyone sitting[162] around him. When we were filled with the joy and rejoicing and gladness of his life-giving words filled with grace, we would go to our dwellings, glorifying God and his servant Abba Macarius, to the glory of the Father and the Son and the Holy Spirit, now and at all times always, forever and ever. Amen."[163]

[162]*Hemsi* can also mean "dwelling."

[163]Beneath this final sentence occurs "Lord, have mercy on your servant Matoi. Amen." Matoi was undoubtedly the scribe who copied the manuscript: cf. n. 127.

CHAPTER THREE

The Life of Saint Macarius of Scetis[1]

THE LIFE OF THE GREAT LUMINARY AND
SPIRITBEARER, PERFECT IN ALL VIRTUE,
ABBA MACARIUS, FATHER AND LEADER OF THE
MONKS OF THE HOLY MOUNTAIN[2] OF SCETIS,
NARRATED BY ABBA SARAPION, THE MOST HOLY
BISHOP OF THE CHRIST-LOVING VILLAGE OF THMOUI[3]
AND DISCIPLE OF ABBA ANTONY THE SPIRITBEARER.
IN THE PEACE OF GOD. AMEN.

Proemium

1   The things that Moses, the servant of God, narrated, in accordance with the law that he received from God for our benefit (for,
according to the written dispensation, it is the law that leads us to
Christ, as the holy apostle said [Rom 10:4]), and also those things
that were written after the law, [47] whether the Judges or the
Prophets or the Kingdoms,[4] or the others (in a word, the Old and

[1]Translated from the text edited by E. Amélineau, "Vie de Macaire de Scété," *Histoire*, 46–117, primarily from Codex Vaticanus LXIV, with variants from other codices
noted. At the top of the *Life* is "The 14th of Epēp [Abib] in the cell [*skēnē*] of Abba
Macarius to the south." Paragraphing and paragraph numbers are my own. Page
numbers in brackets indicate the pagination of Amélineau's text.

[2]Coptic *tōou* can also designate a monastic settlement or community.

[3]That is, Thmuis, modern el-Murda, in the northeastern Nile delta. See Wolfgang
Kosack, *Historisches Kartenwerk Ägyptens* (Bonn: Rudolf Habelt , 1971) 28; "Karte des
koptischen Ägypten" 6B (grid number).

[4]1 and 2 Kingdoms (Septuagint) = 1 and 2 Samuel, and 3 and 4 Kingdoms = 1 and
2 Kings.

New Testaments), are especially profitable, because what is written looks toward a single end, the incarnation of our Savior. For this reason, the ancient Scripture is called law, in accordance with what is written in the Gospels: "Not one letter, or a stroke of a letter, will pass from the law until all these things take place" [Mt 5:18]. Wherefore, since the letter and the stroke of a letter symbolize the cross, these prophecies find their fulfillment in the Lord, who was crucified for us[5] and endured death in the flesh in order to save us and the whole world from the grasp of the Devil [Col 1:22].

Reflecting and meditating on those who themselves became servants of the Word in accordance with the teaching of our Lord (I mean the holy apostles), those whose voice was heard throughout the earth, who became the salvation of the whole world, and reflecting on the others who came after them, who followed in these selfsame godly footsteps and fought with all their might against [48] those drawn up in battle against them in this dream-like existence, who from the beginning looked forward to the imperishable hope that the Savior taught us through his holy teachings in the Gospels, "The road that leads to life is narrow, and few will find it" [Mt 7:14], the holy Spiritbearer Abba Macarius, with admirable zeal, emulated them and followed them; he became worthy to be their companion in word and deed as, indeed, this discourse will reveal to us if I continue. Therefore, insofar as I am able by means of my own words, I will profit those who listen to this account of godliness even if, through the grace of the Lord, I reveal the ascetic practices of the saint only in part.

Macarius' Parents

2   That great Abba Macarius, therefore, according to what we have heard from our fathers who preceded us,[6] came from godly parents

[5]Codex LXII: for all of us.
[6]LXII lacks "according . . . us."

who lived in the service of God and lived their lives in accordance with the holy evangelical law. His father[7] was a priest who diligently served the altar of God with great devotion and his mother was faithful and God-fearing, walking in modesty and continuously worshipping God.[8] [49] The two of them were righteous and Christ was with them. Since they possessed an abundance of life's necessities, they could concern themselves all the more with the salvation of their souls. Their first-born was a daughter and when she had grown up a little, the Lord came to visit her and she passed away from this life. The priest was a lover of God and his blessed wife also; as lovers of purity, they remained at peace[9] apart from their marriage bed for a while after the death of their girl, occupying themselves with prayer, then with fasting and almsgiving and service to the sick. Having become famous for every manner of godliness, they were deservedly loved by everyone. But he who hates what is good, the Devil, could not stand to see them leading such a way of life and being at peace this way but was jealous of them, as is his custom, and so he stirred up temptations against them, one after another, by means of sinful people who were the agents of Satan himself; as a result, they were ruined and all their possessions were scattered.

Abraham, in a Dream, Tells Macarius' Father to Leave for Jijbēr

3   [50] What occurred was similar to what happened to that man who was noble in the ways of God (I am speaking of the righteous Job), for at that time there was no peace in their land.[10] When the

---

[7]Toda Satoshi, "La Vie de S. Macaire l'Égyptien," has observed, 268, that only the Coptic version keeps Macarius' father anonymous while the others call him "Abraham" (see par. 3 below); the Coptic version thus, Toda says, 268, "shows every possibility of being anterior to the other versions of the *Life of Macarius.*"

[8]Throughout the text, "worship" and "serve/service" translate one word in Coptic, *shemshi*, which means both.

[9]-*ēsuchazein*, which normally means "be at peace, in quiet," and is used of the solitary or monastic life.

[10]LXII: in our land. "Peace" translates Gk *katastasis*, which suggests "order,

blessed wife of the blessed priest saw what had happened and was seized by fear, she advised her husband to do something to save their souls, to leave their land and their family, and so it happened. But the priest, because his thoughts were torn, was anxious about all these things and said, "What has happened to me?" Then, when he had gone to sleep that night, he saw in a dream a holy old man, shining brilliantly all over, dressed in the clothing of a patriarch, and when the patriarch drew near to the blessed priest, he said to him, "Do not be afraid. I am Abraham, the father of Isaac who begot Jacob. Therefore, listen to me. Do not disobey[11] the voice of your wife. Leave this land, for God has so decided it. Come, live in Jijbēr.[12] 'I [51] will not forsake you,' says the Lord, 'but I will bless you,' he said [Dt 31:6, Josh 1:5; Gen 17:16, 20],[13] for I too left my country of Haran and I dwelt in the land of Canaan, as the Lord told me: 'And I will give you a son,' said the Lord, 'from this wife whom you now have, and his name will endure for generations[14] with the children that he will beget spiritually to serve me in the place that I will show him' " [Gen 17:15–19, 18:9–15].

When the old priest heard these things, he was greatly astonished but rejoiced all the more as he became persuaded. When morning arrived he called his wife and told her about everything he had seen just as it was told to him. Immediately they were in agreement about what God had ordained. Then they left behind their remaining possessions and left the land where they lived and went to Jijbēr and lived there as they had been commanded in the vision. They secretly took with them a few necessities which were sufficient to buy what they needed.

orderly conditions." Since Macarius was born about 300, perhaps this is a reference to things before the accession of Constantine; Evelyn White suggests, 2.467, that it refers to conditions after the revolt of Achilleus in 295 and its suppression by Constantine.

[11]LXII: "listen to" (*sōtem*) rather than "do not disobey" (*atsōtem*).

[12]A town in the north-central delta; see Kosack, *Historisches Kartenwerk Ägyptens*, "Karte," 4B.

[13]LXII lacks "he said."

[14]Codex LIX: for ever.

An Angel of the Lord Prophesies the Birth of Macarius

4   Therefore, when they were in Jijbēr and, [52] moreover, walked in the commandments of the Lord as was their custom, the clergy of the village, seeing the good character of that old priest, asked him to serve with them in the sanctuary. He, however, in accordance with canonical law, refused.[15] When he[16] had spent a little time there and had established himself, he began to work the earth and to make his living from it since he was a farmer. When some time had passed, he began to grow ill and asked to be taken to the church and slept there in the belief that he would receive healing.[17] While he was keeping vigil at night on account of his illness, he suddenly saw an angel of the Lord[18] standing in[19] the sanctuary and the angel called to him once, twice, and three times, saying, "Get up, come here" [Mt 1:20, Lk 1:11]. But he said to the angel, "I beg you, my lord, truly it is impossible for me on account of the illness I have." When the angel drew near him, he touched him, saying, "It is the Lord who has commanded you to be healed. Get up and stand." And immediately he got up and stood and [53] the angel said to him, "Go to your house and know your wife and she will conceive and bear you a son and he will be a joy to you and his mother and will be renowned for his godliness; as a result, his name will be spoken almost throughout the

---

[15]Macarius' father was probably from another diocese and so would need the permission of the local bishop in order to function as a priest.

[16]LXII: they.

[17]"Incubation," or sleeping in sacred sites in order to obtain healing, was widespread in the ancient world, especially at temples dedicated to Asclepius. The practice also took place in Egypt at the shrines of Serapis and Isis. The most famous Christian example is the pilgrimage site of Saint Menas, Abû Mînâ; see Peter Grossmann, "The Pilgrimage Center of Abû Mînâ," in David Frankfurter, ed., *Pilgrimage and Holy Space in Late Antique Egypt* (Leiden: Brill, 1998), 281–302 and the sources cited on 288 n. 28. Incubation also took place at the shrine of Saint Colluthus; see Lucia Papini and David Frankfurter, "Fragments of the *Sortes Sanctorum* from the Shrine of St. Colluthus," in Frankfurter, ed. *Pilgrimage*, 395 and n. 3 there.

[18]In Lk 1:11 "an angel of the Lord" appears to Zechariah and in Mt 1:20 he appears to Joseph.

[19]LXII: near, beside.

world, for he will bring a people to God to serve him like the angels. They will almost come to resemble the incorporeal in their way of life and worship."

Macarius' Birth and Childhood

5   When the priest awoke from the vision,[20] his wife was in the church serving him and he told her everything. When morning arrived, therefore, they went home and before long the woman conceived, just as the angel had said. She gave birth to a boy and called him Macarius; he was a beautiful child and was filled with grace.

When the boy got older, he would distribute alms daily, in accordance with his parents' instructions, watching them serve God in every way; or rather, they guided him with the help of God's grace, which was with him, for [54] he was a child of the promise, about which we have already spoken. Then little by little he grew strong and so began to help his father with the cares of this life[21] while the Lord God[22] blessed them: he increased the cattle and crops so that everyone marveled at the great abundance in their house.

Macarius is Ordained Reader

6   When, therefore, the villagers saw this young man's situation and the grace of God that shone forth from his face, the clergy of the village laid hold of him and took him to the bishop and urged him to make Macarius a reader, and so it happened. When his father and mother found out, they were grieved once again and said, "The Lord's will be done." Then, when he grew to maturity, his parents were concerned and his mother and father begged him to let them

[20]LXII lacks "from the vision."
[21]LXII: life.
[22]LXII lacks "God."

arrange a marriage for him, but he would not allow it, saying, "Do not trouble yourselves pursuing this matter for me,[23] for the Lord will not agree to this plan." Opposing him as though he were a child, his parents once again begged him to agree to their wishes, having forgotten [55] what had been told them about him. Young man Macarius' whole concern was for God, meditating[24] every day on the Scriptures and books[25] in church and at home; moreover, he reflected on and understood the things he read,[26] pressed into service by the clergy since the Church needed him in its service, and his parents agreed to this.[27]

Macarius, Forced to Marry, Leaves for Scetis

7   Then, although he did not wish it, he was joined to a woman according to human custom, but his heart and his desire were for God, as I have said. He did not touch the woman at all and did not even look at her; rather, when he was thrown together with her, he would throw himself on the bed as though he were ill and in this way he left each day pure and watched over by the providence of God. When the days of his marriage feast had passed, he was made a deacon and he asked his father to release him[28] and allow him to go with his [56] workers[29] and camels to the mountain of natron with the numerous people that went there to transport natron. He did this, then, in order to do away with his concern for his wife and

[23]LXII lacks "for me."

[24]Opposing . . . meditating: LIX His parents opposed him and he followed what they said, while at the same time they looked on him as a child and begged him to agree to their wishes, but he would not agree to this at all, for God was watching over him. His parents had forgotten what was said to them about him, but with his whole heart his desire was for the things of God, meditating.

[25]LXII lacks "Scriptures and."

[26]LXII lacks "reflected on and."

[27]LXII: his parents agreed to this requirement.

[28]LXII: if he could go.

[29]LIX: the workers.

in order not to come into contact with her from that time on. And he did so.

Macarius' Dream

8   At that time large numbers of people from all the villages near Scetis gathered together and thus they were of one heart [Acts 4:32] and went to the mountain and carried out natron on camels, helping one another out of fear of the barbarians who lived within the distant mountain. These barbarians came little by little to the west side of the Nile and made prisoners of those they were able; they seized them and took them to their own land. For this reason, then, since Abba Macarius was himself traveling with company of this sort, it was the custom of the people of his village to call him "Macarius the camel-driver."[30] And so he came one time with a large number of people who were coming in order to transport natron, and they came down upon the outcrop of rock above the valley; when they went to sleep there above the pit so they could later remove part of the natron that they needed, [57] young man Macarius, on account of fatigue, also got drowsy and went to sleep. Later that night he found himself dreaming:[31] a man was standing above him in a garment that cast forth lightning and was multicolored and striped, and he spoke to him, saying, "Get up and survey this rock on both sides and this valley running down the middle. See that you understand what you see!"

"And when I looked," he [Macarius] said,[32] "I said to the person who had spoken to me, 'I don't see anything except the beginning of the wadi to the west of the valley[33] and also the mountain sur-

[30]See *AP* Macarius the Great 31.

[31]Coptic *rasoui*; LXII uses Gk -*horama*, "vision," which is used later on.

[32]The text switches to Macarius speaking.

[33]LXII: to the north of the valley. The Wadi al-Natrun is a well-watered strip of oases about 20–25 miles long that runs in a northwesterly direction. Its southeast end is about 40 miles northwest of modern Cairo.

rounding the valley;[34] I see *it*.' And he said to me, 'Thus says God: "This land I will give to you. You shall dwell in it and blossom and your fruits shall increase and your seed shall multiply [Gen 12:7] and you shall bear multitudes of spiritual children and rulers who will suckle at your breasts; they will be made rulers[35] over the peoples and your root shall be established upon the rock [58] and I will bless the branches of the people that you give birth to from your teachings so they will glorify the Lord God to the ends of the whole earth on account of your good memory. Therefore, arise from sleep and go your way in peace. Heed well what you have heard and what has been told you and afterwards I will appear to you again and, if you have become perfect, I will appear to you and will speak with you face to face," says the Lord God. And see that you do not tell anyone about the vision you have seen for a certain time.' "

Macarius Returns to His Family; His Wife Dies

9   When young man Macarius arose from sleep, and when morning had come, thinking about the things that were said to him and the vision he had seen, he looked like those who are thunderstruck, for he had never experienced something like this. When his companions asked him, "What is this amazing thing that happened to you?"[36] he did not say anything at all.[37] Three days later, he returned home from the mountain of natron and found his wife seized by a

---

[34]LXII: surrounding the wadi.

[35]Gk *hēgoumenoi* can mean "rulers" in general or, more specifically, "monastic superiors." Evelyn White, 2.466, believes that this reference is a "serious anachronism" and refers to "the series of primates who were chosen from among the monks of [the Monastery of] Saint Macarius" beginning with Isaac in the late seventh century, but the term seems to be referring to monastic, not episcopal, leaders.

[36]LIX adds "who are thunderstruck" (-*tomt*), the same word used at the beginning of the paragraph, a variation of which (-*tōmt*) is rendered by "amazing" just previously.

[37]LXII adds "for a while."

very high fever; before it could be reduced, God came to visit her.[38] And [59] when the young man saw what had taken place, he said to himself, "Macarius, show all diligence for the salvation of your soul, for you will also be visited." Since he was pleasing in the Church and loved everyone on account of his great humility, everyone, from the least to the greatest, loved him as their own child and they would all speak about him when they saw his progress and the grace of God that was with him and they would say, "What will become of this young man?" or "When did he acquire this learning?" [Mt 13:54][39] For he did not walk with young people of his age but was friends with gray-haired old men[40] who possessed the wisdom[41] of old age and everyone who knew him would say, "Truly, this young man has the appearance of an angel!"

His father and his mother were delighted with him[42] and when they saw that he loved God so completely, they rejoiced, especially[43] when they found him numerous times on the streets alone[44] praying [60] and again when he was giving alms to those who asked and when he visited the sick. So his parents no longer brought up the subject of his taking a wife or reminded him about it but instead considered his speech God's when they saw the grace that he possessed guiding him from boyhood[45] and nurturing his soul like a foster mother. At last they remembered in particular that he was a promise and they gave him peace in everything. The young man, for his part, when he saw his parents' devotion to God, devoted himself to serving them in everything and obeyed them like a servant before his betters.

---

[38]LXII: and before long she went to her rest in peace.

[39]LIX: this kind of learning.

[40]LXII lacks "old men." See *Life of Antony* 1.2. References to the *Life of Antony* are to G. J. M. Bartelink, *Vie d'Antoine* (SC 400; Paris: Cerf, 1994).

[41]Literally: heart; LXII: form.

[42]"Delighted" renders a phrase with *holj*, "sweet," at its center; sweetness is important in the *Life* and in the *Virtues of Saint Macarius*. LIX lacks "were delighted with him and."

[43]LXII lacks "especially."

[44]LXII lacks "alone."

[45]LIX: childhood.

The Death of His Parents

10   When the young man, in accordance with the laws of nature, reached full adulthood, his father had become an old man, having lost his sight, like the patriarch Isaac [Gen 27:1], and when he became weak on account of his advanced age, he took to his bed and remained there and Saint Macarius[46] waited on him, serving him, asking him at all times in faith to bless him, and so he blessed him [see Gen 27]. [61] When he completed his days in good old age, he stretched himself out and went to his rest and was buried as was appropriate. When his father went to his rest, immediately it came into Macarius' heart to abandon this life with its concerns and to have a single concern and be occupied solely[47] with offering prayer to God without distraction and so he began little by little to distribute everything he owned. But when his mother found out, she spoke to him, just the two of them, and said, "My son, what are you doing? Look, you are just a young man. See that you don't lose what you have lest you be in want and as a result have to go to work for others."

Since he did not want to grieve her heart, he said to her, "I will do whatever you tell me," but in his heart he kept his own counsel.

Six months and a few days later, the Lord came to visit the blessed old woman and when she went to her rest, her body was placed beside the blessed priest.[48]

Macarius Visits an Old Anchorite

11   When blessed Macarius was left alone, multitudes of thoughts surrounded him but he would not confide in anyone. [62] Now when a feast day occurred, his heart told him to invite the needy and the weak and to give alms to them as was his custom in order that

[46]LXII: Macarius; LXIV: blessed Macarius (*-makarios makari*).
[47]LXIV lacks "solely."
[48]Blessed: *-makaria* and *-makarios*.

they might remember his parents. There was an anchorite some distance from his village whose head was covered with hair; he stood in
great fear of God, living a life of quiet[49] in a small monastic
dwelling[50] by himself.[51] When this anchorite happened to be in
church that day because there was no priest in his monastic dwelling
from whom he could receive the blessing,[52] Saint Macarius asked
him also to come receive alms[53] and so he agreed to come. When
they had finished eating, Saint Macarius[54] said to him, "I beg you,
holy[55] father, to let me come see you tomorrow[56] in order to tell you
what is on my mind, for the matter is important."

Since the old man knew Macarius'[57] way of life, he agreed. When
morning arrived, Macarius went to see him and so he told him
everything that was on his mind: "I wish," he said, "to withdraw as
an anchorite and to be occupied with saving my soul." When the old
man saw the grace [63] of God that resided with[58] the young man,
he marveled at his situation and what he had said. Then the old man
took Macarius with him that night in order to know what the Lord
might inform him concerning the young man, for he was a seer.

The Old Man's Vision Concerning Macarius

12   When the sun went down they ate a little bread and the two of
them went to bed and when the old man abstained from sleep God
opened his eyes and he beheld a choir of monks surrounding Abba

[49] -ēsuchazein.
[50] -monē.
[51] In Life of Antony 3.3, Antony visits a village ascetic.
[52] That is, the eucharist.
[53] Literally: the giving of love or charity, ti agapē.
[54] LIX: Abba Macarius the Great.
[55] LXIV lacks "holy."
[56] LXIV: first thing in the morning.
[57] LXIV: blessed Macarius'.
[58] LXIV: in.

Macarius as he slept. The old man saw that[59] they were all white and that all of them were growing wings on their backs like eagles, and he heard a voice saying, "Get up, Macarius, begin your ministry, for the time has come," and "Arise. Go. It is I who send you." When, therefore, the holy old man heard these things, he kept silent for a while and when the light rose, as the blessed Macarius was making to go, the old man said to him, "Didn't you see anything last night?"

He said to him, "No, nothing at all. I had a good night's sleep; my spirit is refreshed."

Then the old man said to him, "That which has risen up [64] in your heart,[60] do; it is the Lord who summons you."

The old man did not say a word about what he saw lest the young man become vain but he ordered him to go immediately[61] in order to go far away and live near another village in the cells for none of the servants of God lived in the interior deserts except Antony the Great who went to the desert places numerous times and returned.[62] When the blessed Macarius went to the village, he quickly began to distribute all his possessions to the poor and weak.[63]

Macarius Lives as an Anchorite Outside a Village; Seized and Ordained Priest

13   [65] And so he left the village. He went to a cell outside another village and lived there by himself for a while. When the villagers

[59]LIX and LXIV lack the beginning of the sentence up to here.
[60]LIX: Then the old man replied, "What has come to your heart."
[61]LXII and LXIV lack "immediately."
[62]See *Life of Antony* 3.2, 11.2.
[63]See *Life of Antony* 2.5. LIX: When Macarius heard these things from the old anchorite, he rejoiced at this counsel. Taking his advice, Macarius, the beautiful athlete, made progress. On account of this, the villagers seized him and made him a priest against his will. This undoubtedly took place according to the divine plan of God so he could help Macarius and the others with him in order to bless them when afterwards they lived in the desert places. Then, since the weight of ordination was a burden to him, he decided to flee from it; as a result, after leaving the old man he quickly began to give his possessions to the poor and weak.

there saw his good character and his gentleness, because they did not have a priest in the village to give them the blessing,[64] they secretly spoke with the bishop about this matter;[65] then they seized him (he did not know their plans) and made him priest against his wishes. Even this happened to him according to divine plan so God might help him and the others with him when later they lived in the desert places. When he lived in that cell many days and profited everyone who came to see him, then the Devil began returning to his original attack; but blessed Macarius was not bothered for a while by thoughts stirred up by the Devil so he remained there, not only so he would not run away from battle but also so he could make the desert a new world of the God of heaven, the place where he would assemble for the Lord an army of spiritual soldiers girded with spiritual armor against [66] the Devil's apostate legions, I mean those beings with defiled spirits and those spiritual soldiers who fight against him—he being the Devil—with the sharpened spears[66] of the virtues, they who have proven victorious over him in the name of Jesus Christ our God. But God, foreseeing and wise, by divine dispensation allowed temptation to rise up against Abba Macarius so that through it he might remember the things that had been told to him and might leave for the desert, the place he had told him about, and might gather around him all those who desired eternal life. That temptation all of you know, since he himself told the story with his own mouth on numerous occasions.[67] Nevertheless, I will tell it to you, brothers.[68]

[64]That is, the eucharist.
[65]Or: about him.
[66]LXII: spear.
[67]LXIV lacks "on numerous occasions."
[68]LXIV lacks "to you, brothers."

A Young Woman Accuses Macarius of Making Her Pregnant[69]

14   There was a young woman in that village who had grown to maturity but had not yet married. There was also a young man in her part of town who was a close relative of hers. Now the young man's parents planned to unite the young woman to their son in respectable marriage [67] according to human laws of nature, but when the two grew up the agreement fell through to marry them to each other[70] on account of the poverty of the young man's parents. A certain freedom, however, developed between the young woman and the young man on account of their kinship and the fact that they lived in the same neighborhood, as we have said above. They met each other a number of times in their homes and on the streets. When a feast day occurred and they drank wine and got drunk, they fell into ruin and the two of them lost their virginity. And so little by little the young woman began to show. The two of them were afraid that their parents[71] would kill them on account of the shame they had brought them[72] and so they devised a plan filled with iniquity, adding another great[73] sin on top of their previous fornication. Each partner said to the other, "What will we do? If our parents find out about it they will kill us, but let's say that the priest, the anchorite, is the one who did it because he's a stranger and no mercy will be shown to him."

And so they did just as they had said. When the parents of the young girl found out that this had happened to her,[74] they asked her, [68] "What has happened to you? Who did this? Tell us!" She, just as she had been instructed by the young man, said, "I went to see the anchorite one day. It was he who did this to me. He got me preg-

[69]A much shorter version of this story occurs in *AP* Macarius the Great 1 (= Coptic *Sayings* 1); Ward, 124–25.
[70]LXIV lacks "to each other."
[71]Or: their fathers (*-ioti*); and below.
[72]LXIV lacks "they had brought them."
[73]LXIV lacks "great."
[74]LIX: that she was pregnant.

nant." So the parents got angry and furious on account of the shame their daughter had brought them and went to the cell along with some others.[75] The crowd brought Abba Macarius out and beat him badly enough to kill him. But the saint, since he did not know about what had happened, asked them, "What has happened that you hit me so mercilessly like this?" Finally they bound to his back some pots smeared with soot and dragged him through the middle of the village, with a crowd of children walking with him, beating him and pulling him this way and that like they do to those who are crazy, all of them crying out about him in a single voice and saying, "He stuck the girl!" (The God-loving man who faithfully served Abba Macarius in order to receive his blessing was shamefacedly walking behind him [69] at that time.)[76]

After Abba Macarius was badly humiliated with blows and mocking words, some of the faithful came from a distance and, when they saw him near death, asked him what had happened to him. And when they understood they said, "What you people are saying is not true. We know from our previous experience with him that this man is faithful and righteous." And they stood around him and loosened the bonds and also broke the pots smeared with soot that had been placed around his neck.[77] And the young man's father said, "Impossible! You can't do that until he guarantees that when the young girl gives birth he will pay the cost of her delivery and provide for the raising of her child." Abba Macarius said, "What an injustice! I do not acknowledge this charge brought against me!" Then the man who served him said to him, "Please, make me the surety."[78] And he became surety for Abba Macarius and so they released him. He returned to his cell half dead.

When he entered his cell, he said to himself, [70] "Macarius, look! You have found yourself a wife. Now the situation requires you

---

[75]LIX: with a number of children. See below.

[76]John the Little also had "a devout layman" to serve him at Klysma; see Mikhail and Vivian, "Life of Saint John the Little," 51.

[77]LXIV: shoulders.

[78]LIX lacks "please."

to work night and day so you can provide for yourself and for her and her child."[79] And so he diligently got to work and he gave the baskets that he made to his servant in order to sell them and give the money he made to the woman so that when she gave birth she could use it for herself and her child.[80] But God, who loves humankind, who glorifies those who give glory to him, who knows things before they occur just like things that have passed, who knows his elect long before they are born [Jer 1:5], did not wish to allow this treasure to be hidden [Mt 13:44]; nor did he wish to keep silent and not reveal the way of life of his servant Macarius but instead decided that everyone should know that there is always hope for the faithful. Therefore, when the time came for that wretched young girl to give birth, the labor pains were severe and difficult. She was in danger of dying for four days and four nights and was not able to give birth. Her mother said [71] to her, "What is happening to you, my daughter? Look, much longer and you'll be dead."

She said, "Truly[81] I deserve to die; not only have I sinned but I have also falsely accused God's servant[82] the anchorite. That holy man did not touch me at all; no, it was such and such young man[83] who got me pregnant." And when that young man heard, he fled so they could not catch him. Moreover, when that wretched girl gave birth after confessing the truth, the servant of Saint Abba Macarius ran to him with great rejoicing and pride and said to him, "That young girl who falsely accused you was not able to give birth until she confessed 'It was not the holy man who did this to me but such and such young man'!"[84] Everyone who heard what had happened came to see Abba Macarius—all of them—glorifying him and

---

[79]LIX: your child. Macarius' work does not seem to jibe with his servant's becoming surety for him, but Gk *enēgguēsato me* (⟨egguan⟩), PG 65.260A, in addition to "answer for someone" (Ward, 125: "vouched for me"), can also mean "become surety for."

[80]LXIV: the child.

[81]LXIV: Yes.

[82]LIX: the servant of the Lord.

[83]LIX: a young man on my mother's side.

[84]LIX: a young man on her mother's side.

greatly praising him. But the servant rejoiced even more because the Lord God had taken away all the shame he had had on his face, for the crowd had upbraided him only a short time before when they heaped contempt on him, saying [72] to him, "Look! The man whom you said was a saint! Look how we found that he was really this and doing that!"

A Cherub Visits Abba Macarius

15   Therefore, when events like these took place, Saint Abba Macarius decided to leave that cell and go someplace else to live. Later, then, on an appointed day when he would receive the holy mysteries alone in his cell, as was his custom, and when he would stand at the altar as was his custom, he looked toward his right and suddenly saw there a cherub[85] with six[86] wings and a large number of eyes. Abba Macarius began to observe him closely, saying, "Who are you?" Then because of the brightness and splendor of the cherub's glory, Saint Abba Macarius fell on his face and became like one dead.[87] When he remained lying on the ground a short while, the cherub took hold of him and revived him and raised him to his feet.

After Abba Macarius came to his senses, the cherub said to him, "Why are you so obtuse?[88] You have disregarded what was said to you on the outcrop of rock and treat everything you heard there as though you were asleep. [73] But you have done well in patiently enduring temptation to the end in order that through your efforts you might learn little by little and be proven in the battles, waged by both demons and people, that the Lord is going to allow to tempt you. Therefore, complete the service you have begun that has been

---

[85]The Coptic, both in the *Life* and in the *Virtues of Saint Macarius*, uses the plural "cherubim" for "cherub."

[86]LXIV: three wings, which must mean "three (pair of) wings." See Is 6:2 and Rev 4:8, where the number is six.

[87]LIX: the dead.

[88]Literally: Why is your heart so completely thick?

entrusted to you[89] and receive the holy mysteries, for they will make you pure and strong, and get ready tonight to leave here[90] quickly and to go live in the place that was shown to you once by our Lord.[91] Only, be resolute and do not neglect the order that has been given to you; I will come to you here tonight and we will leave at night. On account of the heaviness of their sleep, no one will know we are leaving. Do not be afraid of anything: the Lord has commanded me not only to tell you to leave here but also to be with you [74] in the place the Lord has shown you until what you have heard spoken to you is fulfilled. For God has decided to make you the father of a multitude, not through fleshly generation, but by the calling of spiritual children. I have been ordered by God[92] to serve the people that you will gather together in accordance with the decision of my God; I will serve them in secret[93] until the end of days—if, of course, they keep the precepts and commandments of the Lord that you will give them."

And when he had said these things, the cherub spoke once again to him, "I will come to you tonight. Do not be afraid, and do not equivocate, for it is the Lord who commands you. See that you do not oppose him."

Saint Abba Macarius, therefore, comforted and encouraged by the presence of the cherub, forgot all the hardships and difficulties that had been given to him[94] and so he prepared himself to follow everything that had been told him. [75] That night when he arose to perform the *synaxis,* as was his custom, suddenly everywhere became filled with light as at midday in the days of summer; because

[89]For *-leitourgia* ("service"), LXIV has *-diakonia*, and lacks "that has been entrusted to you."

[90]LXII lacks "here."

[91]LIX: Go quickly, therefore, in order to leave this place here that you were first told about.

[92]LXII and LXIV: from on high.

[93]*-mustērion*; see Lampe 892AB. Gk *mustērion* indicates the secret purpose of God or a secret of God revealed by divine activity.

[94]LXII: that he had received.

of the situation, Abba Macarius knew that it was the cherub who had come to him. That power diminished a little before it spoke with Abba Macarius so he would not be shaken, then finally the cherub spoke to him, "Arise, gird yourself with power from God, who gives you power, and follow me to the place which has already been shown you by the Lord."

Abba Macarius Leaves for Scetis

16   And so, leaving behind everything in his cell, he left with joy, being guided by the cherub, or rather, by the power of God. And after two days they entered the mountain and went this way and that inspecting various parts of the mountain; then Abba Macarius said to the cherub, "I beg you, my lord, show me where I will live; I don't recognize anything here."

The cherub said to him, "You are free to choose where you will live. See, the place lies before you; but examine it and take possession of a good site. Only, be on the watch for evil spirits and their evil ambushes, [76] and if you remain steadfast, I will visit you regularly, as I have been commanded by my God."[95]

After Abba Macarius had spent many days searching and traveling about the mountain, he came upon the beginning of the wadi near the site where natron was extracted so that water was not too far from him and he dug in the rock. He made a cave and lived in it for a while. Then he made his way into the desert and lived more quietly there and[96] he went up into the rock that lay to the south. He stayed there because near where the natron was extracted the guards bothered him as they dug up natron where the barbarians killed the soldiers.[97] After spending some time there, he dug two caves in the

[95]See *Life of Antony* 10.1–3; in both, grace (in the form of a ministering angel or cherub) requires human perseverance.

[96]LIX and LXIV lack "and."

[97]This event is not recounted earlier in the *Life.* Evelyn White believes, 2.466, that it refers to the (later) death of Abba Moses and his companions during the first bar-

rock and in one of them he built a tabernacle[98] to the east in order to receive the sacrament there. He would sit occupied with prayer, working at plaiting baskets, and he gave the baskets that he made to the watchmen, who would sell them and bring him [77] his necessities and also fine wheat for making the bread for the holy eucharist.[99]

When the numerous demons there saw the saint's courage and his fervor for God, they became like mad beasts, circling around and around him, but were unable to come near him, for they were no longer allowed to by God. This happened in accordance with God's mercy so Macarius from the beginning would not be disturbed and so he would not be easily discouraged, for no one lived on that mountain who could give him direction and counsel him how to combat the evil thoughts brought on by the impure spirits. When not many days had passed, he said to himself, "This place! I have come here[100] as I was ordered, but there is no one here who will direct me[101] in doing spiritual work like those who live in the desert places. What shall I do? This is what I will do: when I was in Egypt[102] I heard about how Saint Antony [78] lived in the interior deserts a long time.[103] Therefore I will get up and go see him so he may edify me and set my thoughts aright for returning here."

---

barian raid on Scetis in 408 (he reasonably suggests that "soldiers" [*matoi*] refers to monks, as above with "the spiritual soldiers" in par. 13).

[98]-*skēnē*. "Two caves" probably means a chamber used for living quarters and a chamber with the *skēnē*, a chapel.

[99]-*sumetalion* is Gk *simidalion*, from classical Gk *semidalis*, fine or refined flour; *artos semidalitēs* is bread made of *semidalis* for the eucharist (*prosphora*).

[100]LIX: I know it.

[101]LIX: to give me direction.

[102]"Egypt," in contrast to "the desert," here means the Nile delta, where Macarius came from, but can also mean Alexandria and also the area around Babylon (Cairo); in other words, "the world." See, for example, *AP* Macarius the Great 15, 18, 24.

[103]LXII and LXIV lack "long."

Abba Macarius Goes to Visit Saint Antony

17   And he got up and prayed and left. He went to the mountain
where Abba Antony lived.[104] When Abba Macarius met Abba
Antony, the old man received him with great joy and gladness[105] and
when Abba Macarius told him what he was thinking, with frankness
like a child before his father, without keeping anything back, the old
man kissed him on his head and said to him, "Macarius, my child,
you are blessed,[106] just as your name means "blessed." Indeed, the
Savior already told me about you many days before you came to see
me. So I've been expecting you in order to see you safe and sound
and to know your situation."

Then the old man comforted and encouraged him with words
appropriate to monastic thought,[107] showing Abba Macarius all the
ways that the demons waged war [79] against him with overt and
covert thoughts until death "so that you too," he said, "might become
strong if they fight against you." Abba Macarius implored Abba
Antony to let him remain with him but the old man would not allow
it, but said to him, "Let each person remain where the Lord has called
him." And Abba Macarius spent some days there and received counsel daily from Abba Antony and his thoughts were at peace with
returning. While he stayed there, he slept beside me each day—I,
Sarapamōn, the most unworthy—[108] and after the night prayer we

---

[104]If this trip did in fact take place (see *AP* Macarius the Great 4), it would have
been quite a journey, whether it was to Antony's "outer mountain" (*Life of Antony*
11.1), Mt. Pispir, east of the Nile (present-day Deir el-Maimun, just south of Kor-
eimat), about 75 km south of Memphis, half way between present-day Itfih and Beni
Suef or, even further, to Antony's "inner mountain," Mt. Colzim (Qulzum), near the
site of the present-day Monastery of Saint Antony.

[105]LXII and LXIV: with joy.

[106]LIX: you are blessed, you are.

[107]Literally: to the habit (*-schēma*) of monasticism [LXI: the monks]; see Lampe
1359B, 12, 13, 16.

[108]LIX: beside Sarapiōn, the old man's faithful disciple; see the discussion on
Sarapion/Serapion in the Introduction to this volume above.

would bless those who had been victorious in battle and we also told each other the story of our life.[109]

Macarius Returns to Scetis and Fights with the Demons

18 When the saint returned to his place, he sat in his dwelling, occupied only with[110] God and firm in his faith, and the cherub regularly visited him day after day. When [80] evening came one day, he left to get water in the wadi for he had not yet dug cisterns, and while he was still walking, meditating on the Scriptures, a voice suddenly came from heaven, "Macarius! Macarius!" But when he stopped and looked here and there, there was no one around. Once again he heard the voice a third time.[111] Filled with fear, he sat down and the voice said to him, "Since you have obeyed my order and have followed me, look now: I will gather around you here a people from every nation, that they may serve[112] me and that I may be glorified[113] in them through their good works and chosen way of life when my name is blessed by those below. See, therefore, that you do not turn away any of those who come to you."

When he recovered his courage, he got up and resumed his journey, and after he returned to the cave the sun went down and after he ate he slept that night.[114] When he was getting up at his customary time, he heard the demons[115] speaking with one another and saying, "Shall we allow this man to stay here and [81] allow the desert places on account of him to become a port and harbor for everyone in dan-

[109]LIX: we spoke with one another about the greatness of those who have fought in accordance with God and we encouraged each other, revealing our lives to one another.

[110]LIX: blessing.

[111]Each "Macarius!" is apparently taken as one time.

[112]Or: worship.

[113]LIX: be blessed.

[114]LXII lacks "and after he ate he slept that night."

[115]LIX: Praying at night, as was his custom, the Lord opened his ears and he heard the demons. "Opened his ears": see the end of the paragraph.

ger, and especially to become a city like heaven[116] for those who hope
for eternal life? If we allow him to remain here, multitudes will gather
around him and the desert places will not be under our power. What's
worse, they will run us off with the lash of their prayers! Come on,
let's scare him. Maybe we can frighten him away." But Saint Macarius
heard these things. His heart was strong like a lion's;[117] moreover,
within himself he blessed God who had opened his ears so he would
understand how powerless are the impure[118] demons.

When the saint prayed, therefore, the entire congregation of
demons suddenly went above the cave to the top of the rock, like a
troop of horses locked in battle against one another. Others came up
to the door and made balls of fire, hurling them into the cave, then
all of a sudden they dispersed. [82] Saint Macarius was calmly recit-
ing the Psalms, saying, "The Lord is my light and my safety; before
whom shall I be afraid? It is the Lord who fights for my salvation;
before whom shall I be faint-hearted?" and other words after these
[Ps 27:1]. When morning came, he went outside, and no one was
there; going back inside, he sat down to his customary work. And so
he did this every day because the Lord allowed him to be tempted
for a time by thoughts. Therefore the demons would cast wicked
thoughts into his heart. "My thoughts began to be," he said, "like a
table laden with every kind of food to eat: fornication and[119] gluttony, fearfulness and grief, arrogance[120] and vainglory, fear and sor-
row, boastfulness and pride, unbelief and blasphemy and lack of
faith in God, which cuts off every path of godliness; in a word, the
demons fought against me by means of my thoughts with their
whole arsenal of arguments, just as my father Abba Antony had told
me."[121] [82] The Lord, through his providence and grace freely

[116]LIX: larger than heaven.
[117]LIX: like the heart of lions.
[118]LXII and LXIV lack "impure."
[119]LIX adds "and love of vainglory."
[120]"Fearfulness," "grief," and "arrogance" all include *hēt*, Coptic for "heart."
[121]A goodly portion of the *Life of Antony*, 16–43, is given to Antony's teaching
about demons.

extended to the saint, helped him in these battles and Abba Macarius emerged victorious.[122]

Abba Macarius Returns to Visit Saint Antony; Antony's Death

19   When quite some time had passed, with the demons continuing to fight against him by means of these thoughts, he got up and went to Saint Antony. When Abba Antony saw Abba Macarius at a distance, he said to us, his disciples, "Behold, a righteous Israelite in whom there is no deceit [Jn 1:47]; indeed, he will be a branch long and straight[123] and the fruit that grows from his seeds will be sweet in the Savior's mouth. I mean his children and his children's children,[124] who will receive his holy teachings."

When, therefore, Abba Macarius met Saint Abba Antony, he threw himself on his face[125] and venerated Abba Antony on the ground, and when Abba Antony raised him up he greeted him with a kiss. When the old man saw Abba Macarius sad and frail on account of the attacks of the demons, the old man said to him joyfully, "What has happened to you, Macarius my child?"

Abba Macarius said to him, "God has already told you, my father, what has happened to me."

Abba Antony comforted him [84] with a multitude of words and said to him,[126] "Be strong and take courage in what is happening, for God has decided to test you by means of every kind of adverse circumstance so that you too can also help others and encourage them,[127] for you have been called to be the father of many nations who will love the true philosophy of monasticism, as has been told

---

[122]As Antony does in *Life* 14.1.

[123]LIX: like a straight eagle (*achōm*), instead of "branch" (*lachem*), which, as Am points out, makes no sense.

[124]LXII and LXIV lack the first part of this sentence.

[125]LIX: he prostrated himself on the ground.

[126]LIX: and he slapped him on the back and said.

[127]LXII and LXIV lack "and encourage them."

you by the voice of the Lord that came to you when you were going
to draw water."

When Abba Macarius heard these things, while he had not yet
told him any of his thoughts, he was astonished and said to himself,
"It isn't necessary to say anything to the saint, for he already knows
everything in the Spirit."

And when Abba Macarius remained a few days with him until
he received both his blessing and his counsel, he asked him to clothe
him in the monastic habit, for Abba Antony had said to him pri-
vately, "Do not grow weary of coming here; in truth, before long I
will go to the Lord." And when he had prayed at length, he clothed
Abba Macarius in the monastic habit and this is the reason [85] he
is called the disciple of Abba Antony.[128] But Abba Macarius
implored[129] Abba Antony and with tears begged his forgiveness and
asked him to let him stay with him until he had received his final
blessing, and Abba Antony, not wishing to cause him grief, allowed
him to stay with him. Then he asked his forgiveness and the old man
said to him, "In a little while the Lord will give rest to you from the
heavy burden of wicked thoughts and afterwards the demons will
fight you openly, as they do me, but be strong and have courage, the
Lord is with you to help you. Do not be afraid, and look to that
power, I mean the cherub. Do not oppose him in anything so that he
may remain with you until the end as a comfort, as has been commanded both you and him[130] by the Lord."

When Abba Macarius heard these things, therefore, once again
he was amazed and said to the old man, "I beg you, my holy father,
to let me stay with you until I receive your blessing, if you lay aside
the body."

[128] *The Life of Paul, the First Hermit* by Saint Jerome, written in Latin about 377,
names the two disciples who buried Antony (who are anonymous in the *Life of Antony*
91.1, 92.2) as Amathas and Macarius. See *Life of Paul* 1; Paul B. Harvey, Jr., "The Life of
Paul, the First Hermit, by Jerome," in Vincent Wimbush, ed., *Ascetic Behavior in
Greco-Roman Antiquity: A Sourcebook* (Minneapolis: Fortress, 1990), 357–69, at 360.
This Macarius later came to be identified with Macarius the Great.

[129] *Ti ho* can mean both "beg, implore," as here and "pray" as earlier in the sentence.

[130] LXIV and LXII: him.

The old man said to him, "Now is not the time, my child, nor has it yet been determined, [86] but as I have already told you, let each person remain where the Lord has called him." And the old man gave him a staff that he had long had and embraced him and prayed for him. And when our father Saint Abba Antony completed his course, we wrapped his holy body.[131] And our father Saint Abba Macarius returned[132] to his dwelling in the desert and lived there, occupying himself with his acts of worship,[133] giving glory to our Lord Jesus Christ.

Abba Macarius' Community Grows

20 Afterwards[134] numbers of people began to gather around him, one by one, asking him to make them monks and to live beside him and to teach them the way of the Lord. And he received everyone who came to him, just as he had been commanded[135] and he guided all of them, each in his own way, and he placed them beside himself until he taught[136] them God's work and what is edifying and how to work with their hands. So he had them [87] make caves in the rock and cover them[137] with palm branches and trunks and stalks from the wadi, and they lived in them. And some of the brothers he placed beside him as an order of disciples.

The Two Young Romans (Maximus and Domitius)

21 At that time two young men came to him from parts of the Roman Empire, wishing to live in the desert, and these others[138] he

[131]On the two disciples who buried Antony, see n. 128 above.
[132]In the margin of LXIV it reads "The beginning of the second teacher [? *sach*]," and underneath, "Read (the appointed passage)."
[133]Or: service.
[134]In the margin of LXII it reads "Beginning of the second (reading)."
[135]LXII and LXIV lack the part of the sentence up to here.
[136]LIX: until he guided them.
[137]LXII and LXIV: So he had them make caves in the rock with palm branches.
[138]LXII and LXIV: the others.

received and settled. Before long the Lord visited them and they went to their rest. The old man testified that their work pleased the Lord in every way. When those holy young men went to their rest, they were buried beside the cave and when numerous monks lived in that sheepfold[139] near the cave of the saints, the whole area came to be called the laura of the Romans and is called that to this day.[140]

The Demons Attack Again

22 When Saint Abba Macarius saw the eagerness of the multitudes and their love for God and for each other,[141] he gathered them together and with all of them lending a hand [88] they built themselves a small church. The name of Saint Abba Macarius began to be famous and it reached the courts[142] of the emperors on account of the many ascetic practices and healings that the Lord worked through him for his glory. When the demons saw this godliness shine forth and saw the number of souls that the saint helped, and especially his bringing them as a gift to God in order to serve him, they became very angry and came down upon him at midday while he was sitting by himself.[143] After all of them had surrounded him like dogs, they threw themselves at his face and tore at his flesh without restraint so that they covered his whole body with bruises.[144] He

[139]In the *Life of Saint Daniel the Stylite*, the saint's enclosure is also called a "sheepfold."

[140]On the historical and legendary aspects of these two monks, named elsewhere as Maximus and Domitius, and the founding of this Monastery of the Romans (Pa Romeos or Baramus), see Evelyn White, 2.98–104; for the story, see *AP* Macarius the Great 33 (= Coptic *Sayings* 8), and the *Coptic Life of Maximus and Domitius*, in Amélineau, *Histoire*, 262ff.

[141]LXII and LXIV lack "and for each other."

[142]An interesting word: Gk *aulē*, "court, courtyard," then "imperial court" (Lampe, 264B), with a plural Coptic ending, *aulēou*.

[143]This reflects an accurate knowledge of the noonday demon *acedia*, spiritual torpor.

[144]The Coptic presents a particularly striking image here: "bruises" translates *lelechēmi. Lele*, from *aloli*, is a grape, and *chēmi* means "black" (the Coptic for "Egypt"). So Macarius' body looked like it was covered with "blackened grapes," or raisins.

remained prostrate for a while and there was no one to help him; he was scarcely able, with great difficulty, to make it to the church after three days.[145]

When he was healed of these wounds, suddenly the cherub appeared to him and said to him, "The Lord has come to dwell[146] in this place on account of you. Arise now, follow me, and I will show you the place that you will bring to perfection before your death." [89] The cherub led him and took him atop the rock at the southern part of the wadi to the west[147] of the cistern at the top of the valley and said to him, "Begin by making yourself a dwelling here and build a church, for a large number of people will live here after a while."[148] And so he lived there to the day of his death, and after his death[149] they called that place "Abba Macarius" because he finished his life there. Saint Abba Macarius lived there many days[150] and was greatly troubled by the demons, both secretly and openly.

The "Cistern of Abba Macarius"

23   Abba Macarius happened one time to be digging a well with the brothers so they would have water to drink from it. When midday came they stopped working so they could rest a little. He remained alone and washed himself before going inside and the demons came upon him and threw him into the hole and began to stop up the cistern until they reached his navel.[151] [90] When the brothers left and

[145]LXII: he left with difficulty.

[146]*Jōrj, jorj=* can also mean "prepare, provide."

[147]LXII and LXIV: below.

[148]The geography seems obscure here, although the present-day Monastery of Saint Macarius is indeed at "the top of the valley," that is, at the eastern end of the wadi. Of the four monasteries of the Wadi al-Natrun, the sign for Saint Macarius' is the first one that travelers from Cairo on the Cairo-Alexandria highway see.

[149]LXII and LXIV lack "and after his death."

[150]LXII and LXIV: a time.

[151]See Crum 671A s.v. *h(e)lpe.* Göttingen Arabic 114, 22 has "(up) to half his height" or "(up) to the middle of his height." I wish to thank Maged S. Mikhail for

did not see him, they were saying to one another, "What's happened to our father?" And when they came up to him they said to him, "What happened to you?" But he smiled and said to them, "Give me a hand and help me up," and so they lifted him out. And when they had dug the cistern,[152] they drew water from it and they named that cistern "the cistern of Abba Macarius," which name it has to this day because he was thrown down it. Indeed, he dug a number of cisterns with the brothers and not one of them was given the name "the cistern of Abba Macarius" except that one. What is more, after his death numerous healings took place in that cistern.

Abba Macarius Heals the Sick

24   Saint Macarius would be brought numbers of sick people from many places, even from far away lands, too, and he would heal all of them, almost like one of the apostles. Indeed, Antony the Great had already testified about him, "The gift of healing has been given to Abba Macarius by God," and you would find the area around his dwelling filled at all times with those who were sick [91] and those who were possessed by demons. He would heal them by making the sign of the cross on them in the name of our Lord Jesus Christ: the lepers he would purify; the paralytics he would heal, and with a word from his mouth—or, rather, by the power of God—he would send them whole,[153] each one of them, on his way; and the dead he raised. Simply put, nothing was impossible[154] for him because of his great humility and his inextinguishable[155] love for God—or, rather, it was the Holy Spirit who worked all things in him.

supplying the Arabic. Presumably the demons were filling in the cistern with sand or rock.

[152]LXII and LXIV: they returned to the cistern and.

[153] *Toujēout* also means "saved."

[154]Nothing was impossible (*atjom*) for Macarius because he had the power (*jom*) of God with him.

[155]LIX: great.

Abba Macarius Heals a Deaf and Dumb Man Possessed by Satan

25 It so happened that there was brought to him one time a deaf and dumb person in the form of [. . .]¹⁵⁶ who wounded everyone who touched him.¹⁵⁷ It took four men to control him and they were able to bring him to the saint only with difficulty. And when they had brought him to the old man, he said to the people, "Let him go," and when they let him go, immediately the man came towards Abba Macarius, broke the chains around his own neck and his hands, and fled from the mountain, bellowing like a camel. The men said to the old man, "He will find someone and murder him!"¹⁵⁸ The old man prayed secretly and the old man said, "Leave him alone. Do not be afraid."

[92] After going here and there, the man returned once again to them and the old man said to him, "What is your name?"

He said to him, "Satan is my name."

The old man said to him, "In the name of Jesus my God, you shall now leave him and never return to him to the day of his death, for thus says the Lord Jesus!"

The man fell to the ground in front of Abba Macarius and was like someone dead and the holy old man took water and poured it over his face and ears and he also poured it into his mouth for him to drink. He allowed him to sleep beside the men and went inside and prayed to God.¹⁵⁹ When he came out, he took oil from the lights of the sanctuary and placed it in his mouth and likewise on his ears;¹⁶⁰ he touched him and said to him, "Get up and go home." And

---

¹⁵⁶The text *mpatalos* is corrupt. Since "m" is genitival after "form," the presumed Gk word must be *patalos*, which is unattested; *patagos*, "chatterer," might be a possibility, but the demoniac is said to be dumb.

¹⁵⁷LXII and LXIV: who hit everyone with whom he came in contact.

¹⁵⁸LIX: he will succeed in murdering someone!

¹⁵⁹LXII and LXIV: he went inside and prayed.

¹⁶⁰Such oil was also considered efficacious at other holy places, e.g., the shrine of Saints Cyrus and John at Menouthis and the Church of Saint George at Shenoute's White Monastery; for the former, see A.-J. Festugière, *Sainte Thècle, Saints Côme et Damien, Saints Cyr et Jean (extraits), Saint Georges* (Paris, 1971), 228–31, and for the

when he got up, he was able to hear and speak and the demon left him, and he gave glory to God and to Saint Abba Macarius for the miracle that had taken place.[161]

Three Demons Accost Abba Macarius at Night

26   When Abba Macarius was asleep one night,[162] three demons [93] appeared and said to him, "We are saints. Get up so we can pray."

He remained sitting and said to them, "Go to the darkness where there will be tears [Mt 8:12]."

They said to him, "You blaspheme the saints? Get up so we can pray! A demon will not say to a person 'Pray.' But look, there are three of us, a type of the Trinity."

Again, however, he cursed them in the name of the Lord. When they drew near to him, he began to slide himself back with the mat that was under him and cried out, "My Lord Jesus, help me!"[163]

Immediately they became like smoke and disappeared.

The Cherub Again Visits Abba Macarius

27   One day while he was sitting, the cherub there came to him and when Abba Macarius saw him he rejoiced, and the cherub said to him, "Be strong in the contests and in everything give glory to God and watch yourself lest you take pride in these healing powers that you have and your labors be destroyed."

And Abba Macarius said to him, "What do I take pride in, my lord? Look! The demons afflict both my body and my soul with the stench of their impure passions and inside [94] I am like a woman

latter, Janet Timbie, "A Liturgical Procession in the Desert of Apa Shenoute," in David Frankfurter, ed., *Pilgrimage*, 439.

[161]LIX: and everyone gave glory to God for the man's healing.

[162]LIX: one day at midday. See par. 22 above for a demonic attack at midday.

[163]See *AP* Macarius the Great 19 where Macarius advises a monk to simply say "Lord, help!" if the conflict becomes fierce.

who is defiled by her menstruation. And how shall I be proud? My experience tells me that the Lord Jesus Christ is the one who is my help and that it is his grace that works the healing."

Abba Macarius and the Men on the Island[164]

28   Later, when that holy old man Saint Abba Macarius was living a solitary life of quiet, he was thinking to himself, "I will leave the interior wadi and I will see whether there is anyone before me in the desert places."[165] He delayed while he struggled with this thought[166] for five years. Then he said to himself, "I will get up and I will walk into the interior wadi and I will see whether I find anyone there, as I have been moved to do."[167] So the old man Saint Abba Macarius left and walked four days and when he came upon a lake he saw an island in the middle and when he went to the island he looked and beheld some men who were naked whose skin had become coarse and thickened due to the air and whose hair and nails had grown long. They had become so changed that when he looked at them he trembled, saying, "They're spirits."

[95] But they, when they saw that he was so afraid he was about to fall down, greeted him in the name of the Lord. He, when he recovered his courage,[168] spoke to them and they said to him, "Why have you come?" and "Where have you come from?" and "Who are you looking for?"

---

[164]See *AP* Macarius the Great 2 (= Coptic *Sayings* 21).

[165]On this motif see the story of Abba Pambo in Tim Vivian, *Journeying into God* (Minneapolis: Fortress, 1996), 25–36.

[166]Literally: this thought fought with him.

[167]Just above, Macarius was going to *leave* (*ebol chen*) the interior wadi, while here he intends to travel *into* (*echoun*) the interior wadi. Actually, since the monasteries are located in the interior of the wadi, he would have presumably been moving to the outside, toward the desert, but in early monastic literature such journeying away from the Nile is seen as a journey to the interior.

[168]LIX, from "beheld" to "courage," has a number of variants, mostly in word order, with the same meaning.

He said to them, "I have found what I am looking for and the Lord has not deprived me of it, namely, your blessing."

When he drew near them, he took hold of them to see whether they were spirits and when he realized that they were holy men he venerated them. They looked at him and he asked them about a number of things. They said to him, "We did not live in a monastery in the desert and we have never seen the monastic habit like the one you are wearing, but when we all agreed, we came here, a very[169] long time ago, and since we came here we have not encountered anyone from this world [96] except you. While we were walking together in this mountain, we saw numerous animals of many different kinds; we encountered the people of the mountain many times, and through the Lord's help none of them bothered with us[170] or harmed us, and just as you see us walking now naked, so it is in every season: we do not suffer either in the summer or in the winter, for it is the Lord who has divinely ordained this way of life for us."

And when they asked him about the world and the things of the world, he answered them, "Through God and your prayers, the Lord cares for them through his providence."[171]

When he received their blessing, he left them and returned to his dwelling.

Abba Macarius Grows Old; the Attacks of the Demons Slacken

29   But Saint Abba Macarius began to grow old and his strength[172] began to leave him, but his soul flourished every day in the service of God; overflowing with love for God, he was fearful before the demons so that through the numerous afflictions that they brought

---

[169]LXII and LXIV lack this word.

[170]LIX: touched us. The "people of the mountain" are apparently being differentiated from those "in the world."

[171]See Coptic *Saying* 21 above and n. 72 there.

[172]*Jom* also means "power," an important word in the *Life*.

upon him they began to cease girding themselves for battle against him.[173] [97] When, therefore, they gathered around him one time when he was in the wadi gathering palm branches apart from the brothers, they grabbed the sickle in his hand and when they had seized it they held it high up over him as though they were going to bring it down upon him. But Abba Macarius, his heart as strong as a lion's, cried out at them in a loud voice, "If the Lord has given you the authority to do so, then bring the sickle down upon me, but if not, then go off to the darkness!" And they gathered together and cried out at him, saying, "You are powerful, Macarius![174] From now on we're through with you because all the suffering that we've endured fighting against you has been for nothing. We've gained nothing at your expense!"

He said to them, "It is not my own power that does these things but the grace of the Lord." And so they disappeared and from that day the Lord began to give him rest from the majority of the attacks of the demons and, in place of the many wars that troubled him without ceasing, he gave him calm and abiding consolation, yet not without suffering, for suffering did not leave his heart until the day of his death, but each day he thought, "Is temptation coming?"[175] [98] Thus he was vigilant all the time in accordance with the great discernment that the Lord had graced him with from his youth.

The Saint's Many Disciples

30 When the saint became old, he was asked by multitudes to clothe them in the monastic habit so they might receive his blessing, and so it happened. There were with him multitudes of disciples but they were not all with him. Some of them, zealous with this good

[173]I have translated this sentence literally because I am not quite sure of its meaning.

[174]LXII and LXIV lack this sentence.

[175]In *AP* John the Little 13 (Ward, 87) John discovers, after having all temptations removed from him, that it is good to have afflictions because they bring progress.

zealousness their whole lives, lived far from him in numerous other
places and when others came to live beside them they gave their
names to other monasteries: that of John the Little, and Abba Pishoi,
the disciples of Abba Amoi, the disciple of Abba Pithou.[176] Saint
Abba Macarius rejoiced with gladness when he saw his branches
grow numerous and his seed blossom and when he saw the fruitful-
ness of the spiritual trees that he had planted in the vineyard of the
Lord Sabaoth; he gave glory to God with thanksgiving and said to
himself, "The Lord has fulfilled everything that was told me before-
hand, and with my own eyes I have in part seen them come" [1 Cor
13:12], [99] for it was not only Egyptians who lived in that desert but
people congregated around him from many countries: Rōmania[177]
and Spain, Libya and the Pentapolis, Cappadocia and Byzantium,
Italy and Macedonia, Asia and Syria and Palestine and Galatia; in a
word, his eyes beheld those whom he had been told about before-
hand and it was fulfilled close to his own heart.

The Demons Test Abba Macarius Again in His Old Age

31 When Abba Macarius was old and had lost his strength, the
demons wanted to test him and when he had been brought out to sit

[176]On the ancient Monasteries of Saint John the Little and Saint Bishoi and their
founders, see Evelyn White, 2.106–18. The Monastery of John the Little was abandoned in the 15th century while Deir Anba Bishoi is thriving today; on these monasteries, see Otto F.A. Meinardus, *Monks and Monasteries of the Egyptian Deserts* (rev.
ed.; Cairo: AUC Press, 1992), 48–143, and Tim Vivian, "The Monasteries of the Wadi
Natrun, Egypt: A Personal and Monastic Journey," *American Benedictine Review*, 49:1
(March 1998): 3–32, repr. in Vivian, *Words to Live By: Journeys in Ancient and Modern
Monasticism* (Kalamazoo: Cistercian, forthcoming).

[177]*Rōmania* designates the Roman Empire, but here seems to indicate a specific
locale (it is the first name, prefaced by the feminine article *ti*, in a list of names, all
with the feminine direct article and joined by *nem*, "and"). It would not be modern
Romania, which was then called Dacia. "Romania" as a name for the empire came into
use in the fourth century; see F. Paschoud, *Roma Aeterna: Études sur le patriotisme
romain dans l'Occident latin à l'époque des grandes invasions* (Rome 1967). I wish to
thank H. A. Drake for this reference.

in the courtyard and the sun had gone down, he stretched himself out as though to sleep.[178] The demons came up to the door outside and, since they were a multitude, took on the form of people asking for charity; they knocked, imploring him, "Please show us charity." When he recognized their voice, he deliberately threw himself on the bed and each demon said to his companion, "He's asleep!" and others said, "Maybe he's dead! Let's relax and not worry about him from now on. His soul is as strong as diamond [100] and he's made our efforts futile. Look at all the sufferings that we have brought upon him; they haven't slowed him down. Come, he's dead, let's rest from the storms he has stirred up; perhaps after his death this place will fall apart and after these saints[179] leave will become desert again, like it was before they came."

But Abba Macarius, hearing these things, kept silent while continuously praying and those demons, distressed by the disturbance all around them, took rocks and pounded on the door, but even with this racket he did not pay any attention to them. Finally, they took rocks and threw them into the courtyard; because the Lord was watching over him, none of the rocks came close to him but he remained lying down on the bed as though he were asleep and each of them said, "Truly, Macarius has died!" And they began to weep as though rejoicing over his death and they cried out with joy. When some of the brothers heard, they ran toward the sound of the voices to see what was happening. Then the saint got up and stood and said to the demons, "May the Lord condemn you and completely obliterate your nation from the face of the earth!"

[101] The demons took hold of sand and threw it into the air, crying out, "Once again you have defeated us, you criminal[180] old man!"

And when the victor of light[181] rebuked them in the name of the Lord, they were scared off like locusts.

---

[178]LIX: the blessed old man stretched himself out and went to sleep.

[179]LIX: these men (or: people).

[180]-*kakourgos*; LXII and LXIV have -*kakogeros* (= Gk *kakogēros*), "wicked, evil" old man.

[181]LXII and LXIV: he.

When his strength began to leave him, the brothers implored him to rest a little from the numerous labors that he imposed upon himself and he would say to them, "In just a little while everything will be completed, but I give thanks for your frankness, for I know the love that you have in your hearts for me in my illness, truly I do."[182]

Abba Macarius Heals Agathonicus' Daughter[183]

32   He was sitting one day[184] preparing to eat as the sun was about to set when one of his disciples came in and spoke to him like this:[185] "Sir, a nobleman is outside. He has a child with him, and they are dressed like those who seek charity."

And he said to them,[186] "What do they want? Who are they looking for?"

The disciple said to him, "I don't know what they want or who they are looking for."[187]

The old man said to him, "Bring them in."

The disciple left and told them, [102] but they did not come in.[188] Then the old man went out and when he knew in the Spirit who they were, he said to his disciple, "Go." And he sat down and said to the man, "Who are you looking for?"

The man said, "This child is my son. A demon rules over him[189] (thus the demon says, 'I am the commander of the legions') who

---

[182]LXII and LXIV: I see the love in your souls.

[183]A shorter version of this story can be found in the Coptic *Sayings of Saint Macarius* 7 and *Virtues of Saint Macarius* 3.

[184]LIX: one night. Neither the *Sayings* nor the *Virtues* mentions the time of day.
[185]LXII and LXIV lack "to him like this."

[186]As Am notes, 101 n. 11, the plural pronoun indicates that although one monk spoke to Abba Macarius, others had come in with him.

[187]LXII and LXIV have the monk responding: They wish to receive your blessing.

[188]LXII and LXIV: they were not allowed to come in; or: they (the monks) did not allow them to come in.

[189]*eouon ouarchontikon nemaf;* on *archontikon,* see Lampe 241A. In the parenthesis that follows, "commander" translates *-archon.*

beats him four or five times a day, cutting him. I took him to a number of holy men in my country but they did not heal him. He tears at his clothes and eats his own flesh; therefore I've dressed him in these old clothes."

The old man said to him, "How you have dared to bring this young man to this desert place! As if that were not enough, you have also lied to the Spirit of grace, for this is the daughter of Agathonicus, the procurator of Antioch. You have secretly come with her here with a great parade of soldiers; you have now left them behind the mountain on the road[190] and have brought her here in this get-up so no one will recognize you. And you have done well on account of the offense she would cause."[191]

When he heard these words, the man trembled [103] and threw himself on his face before the old man's feet. Then the saint said to him, "Get up. Do not be afraid. And do not lie again."

The man said to him, "I beg you, my lord, I am a servant of this young woman and, just as her father commanded me, I have brought her here from my country, for I have been sent by her father."

The old man called and they brought him oil and he stood and prayed over both the young girl and the oil and after he made the sign of the cross on her forehead and her ears, he returned her to him healed and said to him, "When you reach your companions, do not stop on this mountain tonight on account of the number of women riding with you, but go nearby to Egypt[192] until your animals recover their strength and your people also. See now, on account of her father's faith in the saints and on account of his orthodox faith in the fathers and in Orthodoxy, the Lord has granted the young woman healing and you will see for yourself that she is healed before you reach your country."

[190]-*strata*, interestingly, from Latin *stratum*.

[191]As on Mount Athos in Greece today, women were not allowed in the monastic community. See Macarius' orders below.

[192]See n. 102 above.

The man called some others of his fellow servants who were standing at a distance; they brought him a bag containing four [104] thousand gold coins. The man took it and offered it to the old man, saying, "I beg you, my lord and father, to accept from my lord this small gift of four thousand gold coins for you to distribute to the poor."

But Abba Macarius said to him, "My child, the Lord's gift is not given for a price, nor do we have any need for something like this here. But go in peace to those who sent you."

The man left him and kept the words of the old man and did not sleep on the mountain until he reached[193] Egypt and when he saw for himself that the girl was healed, he returned to his country rejoicing and giving glory to God.[194]

Abba Macarius' Final Days

33   What we have related up to this point will be sufficient for us, for it would be impossible to recount the mighty deeds and healings that the Lord worked through Abba Macarius and his many ascetic practices, [105] especially those works of his that have been written in other books.[195]

Saint Abba Macarius became greatly weighed down by illness on account of his number of years and his flesh almost perished on account of the labors that he secretly gave himself; to the day of his

[193]LXII and LXIV: went to.

[194]LIX adds the episode of Macarius' encounter with the disciple of Hieracas (see *LH* 17.11 and, for a much longer version, *Life of Macarius of Egypt* [Coptic Palladiana] 6 in the companion volume to this one, *Four Desert Fathers*), then adds: Moreover, there are numbers of other exceedingly great wonders and numerous healings that God graced him with that we have not written about at length in this book because they are written in the book of his ascetic deeds that was set forth by the man of God Saint Jerome. One MS. (a) of the *Life of Macarius of Egypt* has this statement.

[195]A similar statement occurs in the *Life of Macarius of Egypt* (Coptic Palladiana) 11; see *Four Desert Fathers*.

death he did not allow anyone to know everything about his ascetic practices nor all the details of his work, for he zealously protected himself from human honors, just as he had been commanded by the cherub who spoke to him from the beginning.

Finally, his eyes began to grow dim and ceased to work on account of his many ascetic practices and old age, for he was more than ninety-seven years old and about to die. At this time little by little he lost his strength and began to sleep all the time. He would stagger going outside and coming inside. When the brothers gathered around him in a circle, he would comfort them one by one, each according to his need, and would say to them, "The Lord knows that all this time that I have been with you I have not hidden myself from you in order not to tell you what is good for your souls, for I tried not to be a stumbling block for either the great or the little, [106] nor have I ever slept when there was a disagreement between myself and anyone. My conscience tells me that I have never denigrated any godly work that offered me correction. The Lord knows my love for God and my companions and God knows my love for all creation, and the Lord himself is my witness that to this day I have meditated on what he said to me one time: 'You have not yet reached the level of the faithful women who in many places practice your way of life."[196] And even with regard to all the victories that I have gained over the demons, His Grace knows that I have never believed that I did anything by my own power. No, the power of his strength and mercy and help have been my helpers. Finally, my brothers, persevere and be vigilant, for in a little while Macarius will pass away."

When the brothers heard these things, especially when they saw his weakness, they cried out to heaven and wept because he was going to leave them behind and go away and leave them orphans[197] and once again he encouraged them to be silent and said to them, "The time has not yet come, [107] so why are you weeping and griev-

---

[196]See the Coptic *Sayings of Macarius* 33 for this sentence and the story that goes with it.
[197]See *Life of Antony* 88.3.

ing my heart? For it is impossible for this not to happen to each one
of us in his own time, as God ordains."

Saints Antony and Pachomius Visit Abba Macarius

34   And when he had said these things, he was scarcely able to persuade them to be quiet and they got up and left, each withdrawing
to his own dwelling. When the brothers had gone once again, weakness overcame him and he entered the cave by himself and lay down
to sleep. It was one in the afternoon. And while he was thinking to
himself, as was his custom, about his passing away and his meeting
God and the judgment that would be passed against him at that time
and the place where he would be thrown, two saints suddenly
appeared to him, shining brightly with glory and honor, their faces
full of joy. When the old man saw them, he kept silent for a while and
one of them said to him, "Don't you know who I am?"

Although he studied him, he was unable to clearly make him out
on account of the great radiance that shone from him. After a little,
he said to the one who had spoken to him, "I think you're my father,
Abba Antony."

Saint Abba Antony said to him, [108] "Don't you know who this
other person is?"

Once again he was silent, for he never replied to anything hastily.

Abba Antony said to him, "This is my brother Pachomius, the
father of the monks of Tabennesi. We have been sent to summon
you.[198] Hereafter take care of your business, for in another nine days
you will lay aside the garment of skin [Gen 3:21] and you will dwell
with us. Lift your eyes to heaven and see the place that has been prepared for you in order for you to rejoice and enter into rest." And so
the saints withdrew from him.

---

[198]Sisoës, Macarius, and Amoi similarly visit John the Little; Mikhail and Vivian,
"Life of Saint John the Little," 54.

The holy old man kept silent, not wishing to speak to anyone lest people be saddened and his spirit be troubled by them, for he looked at everything like a commander-in-chief surrounded by his soldiers. If soldiers lack such a one (I mean the commander-in-chief), the entire company acts like they have had their heads cut off and, headless, are unable to draw up in battle formation or march into battle. This was especially true [109] for him, for he was like God for the entire nation of monks.[199] After God all of them looked at him as though looking in a mirror and their souls grew strong through his encouragement.

The Death of Abba Macarius

35 He lay on his mat, as was his custom, no longer able to get up on account of the weight of his illness, because he suffered from fever; then, little by little, he lost his strength. On the night when his illness was moving from the eighth to the ninth day, as Abba Antony had said, which was the 27th of Phamenoth,[200] suddenly that cherub, who had remained with him from the beginning, came with large multitudes of incorporeal choirs and said to him, "Hurry, come, for all those standing around you will testify on your behalf." And Abba Macarius said in a loud voice, "Lord Jesus, my soul's beloved, receive my spirit!" [Acts 7:59] And so he went to sleep.

To be sure, there was not a crowd of brothers with him at that time, nor did they know that he would die that day, for he was happy just as he was every day, encouraging the brothers. But when all the brothers heard about his death, they all wept and were heavy-hearted there in the desert that had been prepared for them. [110]

[199]See the Coptic *Sayings of Macarius* 22 (*AP* Macarius the Great 32; Ward, 134), and *Virtues of Saint Macarius* 1 and 32, where the same thing is said about Abba Macarius.

[200]27 Barmahat = 5 April, the feast day of Saint Macarius the Great in the Coptic Orthodox Church.

The brothers who lived in the holy desert places had also been completely guided by him on the road to the full[201] practice of virtue; like a commander-in-chief, he armed them with all the armaments needed to fight against the Devil, that shameless tyrant, and his evil cohorts.[202] From that time on he established them upon the immovable foundation that is Christ our God [1 Cor 3:11], who also protected them at all times and made them invincible through his exalted grace that he poured upon them through the prayers of our holy father Abba Macarius the Great.

When these brothers heard, therefore, that the saint had left the body, they left their dwellings, mourning and grieving over the passing away of him who had been taken away in righteousness to the heavenly habitations on high where he now danced with the angelic powers of heaven whom, moreover, he had emulated in word and deed through the angelic deeds that he manifested in his holy life, admired by those whom he taught and guided, all those who wished to live in accordance with the complete truth of the holy gospel. Therefore, when they at last reached the church, all of them weeping bitterly [111] because they had been robbed of their father this way— to all of them he had been a subject of emulation and encouragement in the anchoritic life and in other good works—they threw themselves upon his holy body for a long time, all of them bitterly wailing.

The Burial of Abba Macarius; Abba Paphnutius Assumes the Fatherhood

36 Afterwards, they performed the appointed liturgy and they offered up over his honored remains the bloodless sacrifice, the body and blood of our Lord Jesus Christ. To conclude, they placed his holy

[201]LXIV lacks "full."

[202]Coptic -*noumeron* represents, via Greek, Latin *numerum. Numerus* was the generic name for any military unit but was used more specifically of units formed in non-Roman areas such as Egypt.

body in the cave beside the church that he had built and went to their dwellings in great mourning because they had been deprived of him who nourished their souls in the fear of the Lord, accompanied by the holy man Abba Paphnutius, who was the greatest of the saint's disciples. It was he, moreover, who assumed the fatherhood in the holy places after Abba Macarius, for he too was a holy man and had pursued the same course as the holy man Abba Macarius the Great.²⁰³ On account of this, he too became famous everywhere. Numbers of monks came to him, not only from Scetis but from nearly the whole land of Egypt, receiving from him every kind of virtue that he naturally possessed on account of the diligent guidance [112] he had received from this truly righteous and perfect man, Abba Macarius the Great.

The People of Jijbēr Take Abba Macarius' Body to Their Village

37   Some time later, the people of Jijbēr found out where the saint's body had been laid (Jijbēr was the saint's village, as we made clear at the beginning of the narrative) and they came down to Scetis secretly, without anyone knowing about them, and they took the body of our blessed²⁰⁴ father to their village, as they had agreed; when they had reverently prepared him for burial they made a great casket of costly wood and so they placed his holy body in it.²⁰⁵ A few days later, they built a *martyrion* southwest of the village (but first they obtained God's approval and the advocacy of the saint), and when they had magnificently adorned it and completed it on the thirteenth of Abib,²⁰⁶ they sent for the holy bishop who was presiding at that time and asked him to consecrate the building [113] and

²⁰³The *Virtues* and *Sayings* of Macarius also refer to this Paphnutius as the disciple of Macarius.

²⁰⁴-*makarios.*

²⁰⁵LXII: After a while, the people of Jijbēr came and took his precious remains and reverently placed them in that village.

²⁰⁶20 July.

he brought with him a large number of bishops. They fittingly completed the appointed liturgy and offered up the holy sacrifice and administered to the entire multitude from the holy body and blood of our Lord Jesus Christ on the fourteenth of Abib.[207] After the holy service they buried the body of Saint Abba Macarius, the righteous and just man, to the southeast of the holy place, having spread the word about his holy body whose great power and miracles and numerous healings continue up to this day through the power of the great God that abides with his holy servant Saint Abba Macarius. Finally, after they spent that whole night saying psalms and benedictions and spiritual songs [Col 3:16] in accordance with the appointed rite, the multitude of holy bishops who were assembled to consecrate the shrine of the truly great Saint Abba Macarius went to their dwellings in peace, giving glory to God.

Peroration

38   You listeners, who love teaching, what we have told up to here reveals to us [114] only a part of the glorious works of our righteous father; nevertheless, learn from this partial account what sort of life this man lived who was perfect in righteousness, for to be sure we have deliberately omitted a large number of signs and wonders, or the numerous healings that God worked through him, in order that the discourse not grow exceedingly long. Perhaps it will be thought that the truth is a lie on account of the exceeding greatness of his works,[208] which are astonishing, for truly he was so completely exalted that we are unable to find anyone who was his equal or who, indeed, is said to have been greater than he.

Who, then, resembled him at that time in his exalted ascetic practices and his scrupulous faith or, moreover, in his longing for God and in his conscience that was pure with regard to everyone?

[207]21 July.
[208]See *Life of Antony* Preface 3.

Who, moreover, was like him in his many acts of humility? With them he broke and destroyed all of the Enemy's powerful weapons and scattered his armor made strong with the weapons of the navel of his belly, just as the Lord said in the presence of Job, that great man, when he told him about the Devil, that his power is in his loins and his strength in the navel of his belly [Job 40:16 (LXX)];[209] [115] he was destroyed by this saint and was run off through the power of God that he possessed. Who, moreover, bridled the evil beast—that is, anger—like he did? Or who demonstrated gentleness for everyone equally like this saint? Who, moreover, slew arrogance, which is abominable to God, like this man, or pride, which overthrows the soul's noblest sensibilities, like this blessed[210] man? To be brief, who destroyed all the works of the Enemy like this righteous man and showed that in the Devil's hands these works were shameful and obscene and life-destroying? Indeed, through his numerous intercessions and abundant tears, he drove away, with the help of the Almighty, all the false teaching of that tyrant the Devil.

Therefore, when we hear these things, my beloved, let each of us evince in himself this same zeal for perfecting this kind of faith until the end as we behold today [116] the way of life of this perfect man— I am speaking about our blessed[211] father. Let us bear for God the fruits of the Spirit [Gal 5:22], like those we have seen in his admirable life (keeping, like painters, their images before our eyes at all times), and with these images in mind let us produce fruits that are fitting for the godly life to which Christ our God has called us through both the advocacy of our holy father and his teaching. With regard to those things in which he guided us, he enlightened us by his natural disposition for the godly virtues. Indeed, he himself was an apostle for his time[212] and he was not inferior to those great men Peter and John, the holy apostles, in anything that we saw with our eyes and

---

[209]Behemoth's "strength is in its loins, and its power in the navel of its belly."
[210]-*makarios.*
[211]-*makarios.*
[212]LXIV: for our time.

have heard from other faithful witnesses, things that now can be expressed only in part. But even a partial recounting of all these things is exquisite in God's sight. So then, may one of us now, with an eye toward doing good, make an offering to God by showing compassion with all his ability; may another person offer a love of God and a loving heart for his companions; may another [117] offer asceticism apart from humankind; another good vigil with moderation and watchfulness; one pure prayer; another a truthful tongue; one purity of body and soul; another abstinence and a clear conscience towards everyone, being a stumbling block to no one, lest his worship be defiled.

To be brief, let each of us be prepared to do those things we have just now spoken about, that our blessed[213] father may see this good fruit that is coming to fruition in us and shining forth in our lives at all times, that he may intercede for us with Christ, beside whom he now stands, that we too may ourselves be reconciled with him in the places that he has prepared for us in the everlasting kingdom of heaven, those places that are prepared for us with him, by the grace and mercy and love for humankind of our Lord and God and Savior Jesus Christ, to whom belongs all glory and honor and all adoration, to the Father with him, and with him the life-giving and consubstantial Holy Spirit, now and at all times and forever and ever. Amen.

[213]-*makarios.*

Index of Scripture Cited

Index of Names

Index of Subjects

Bibliography

Amélineau, É. *De Historia Lausica, quaenam sit huius ad Monachorum Aegyptiorum historiam scribendam utilitas.* Paris, 1887.

———. *Histoire des monastères de la Basse-Égypte.* Annales du Musée Guimet, 25; Paris: Leroux, 1894.

Athanasius. *Life of Antony*, ed. G. J. M. Bartelink, *Vie d'Antoine.* SC 400; Paris: Cerf, 1994.

Bammel, C. P. "Problems of the *Historia Monachorum*." *Journal of Theological Studies*, N.S. 47.1 (1996): 92–104

Bareille, G. "Hiéracas," *Dictionnaire de spiritualité catholique*, 6. 2359–61.

Bartelink, G. J. M., ed. *Palladio: La Storia Lausiaca.* Milan: Fondazione Lorenzo Valla, 1974.

Basil of Caesarea. *Saint Basil: The Letters*, trans. Roy J. Deferrari. Cambridge Mass.: Harvard University Press, 1950.

Bell, David N., trans. *The Life of Shenoute by Besa.* Kalamazoo: Cistercian, 1983.

Bouyer, Louis. *The Spirituality of the New Testament and the Fathers*, Vol. 1: *A History of Christian Spirituality.* Minneapolis: The Seabury Press, 1963.

Brakke, David. *Athanasius and the Politics of Asceticism.* Oxford: Clarendon, 1995.

Brown, Peter. *The Making of Late Antiquity.* Cambridge, MA: Cambridge University Press, 1978.

———. "The Rise and Function of the Holy Man in Late Antiquity." *Journal of Roman Studies*, 61 (1971): 80–101. Reprinted in Brown, *Society and the Holy in Late Antiquity*, 103–52. Berkeley: University of California Press, 1982.

———. "The Saint as Exemplar in Late Antiquity," in John Stratton Hawley, ed., *Saints and Virtues.* Berkeley: University of California Press, 1987.

———. "The Rise and Function of the Holy Man in Late Antiquity: 1971–1997." *Journal of Early Christian Studies*, 6.3 (1998): 353–376.

Bunge, Gabriel. *Evagrios Pontikos: Briefe aus der Wüste.* Trier, 1986.

————. "Évagre le Pontique et les deux Macaires." *Irénikon,* 56 (1983): 215–27, 323–60.

————. " 'Priez sans cesse': aux origines de la prière hésychaste." *Studia Monastica,* 30 (1988): 7–16.

————, and Adalbert de Vogüé, *Quatre ermites égyptiens: D'après les fragments coptes de l'Histoire Lausiaque.* Spiritualite Orientale 60; Begrolles-en-Mauges: Bellefontaine, 1994.

Burton-Christie, Douglas. *The Word in the Desert: Scripture and the Quest for Holiness in Early Christian Monasticism.* New York and Oxford: Oxford University Press, 1993.

Cassian, John. *The Conferences,* trans. Boniface Ramsey. Ancient Christian Writers, 57; New York: Paulist, 1997.

Chaîne, M. "La double recension de l'Histoire Lausique dans la version copte." *Revue de l'orient Chrétien,* 25 (1925–1926): 232–75.

Clark, Elizabeth A. *The Origenist Controversy: The Cultural Construction of an Early Christian Debate.* Princeton: Princeton University Press, 1992.

Coquin, René-Georges. "L'évolution de la vie monastique." *Dossiers Histoire et Archéologie* [*Chrétiens d'Egypte au 4e siècle: Saint Antoine et les moines du désert*] 133 (December 1988): 60–65.

Cotelerius (Cotelier), J.-B. *Ecclesiae graecae monumenta* III. Paris, 1686.

Crum, W.E. *Coptic Ostraca from the Collections of the Egypt Exploration Fund, the Cairo Museum and Others.* London: Egypt Exploration Fund, 1902.

————. *A Coptic Dictionary.* Oxford: Clarendon, 1939.

Daley, Brian E. *The Hope of the Early Church: A Handbook of Patristic Eschatology.* Cambridge: Cambridge University Press, 1991.

————. *On the Dormition of Mary: Early Patristic Homilies.* Crestwood, N.Y.: St Vladimir's Seminary Press, 1998.

————. "What did 'Origenism' Mean in the Sixth Century?" in *Origeniana Sexta,* ed. Gilles Dorival and Alain Le Boulluec, 627–38. Leuven: Peeters, 1995.

Daniélou, Jean. "Les démons de l'air dans la Vie d'Antoine," in Basilius Steidle, ed., *Antonius Magnus Eremita, 356–1956: Studia ad Antiquum Monachismum Spectantia,* 136–147. Studia Anselmiana, 38; Rome: Herder, 1956.

Descoeudres, Georges. "L'architecture des ermitages et des sanctuaires," in *Les Kellia: Ermitages coptes en Basse-Egypte*, 33–55. Geneva: Musée d'art et d'histoire, 1990.

Draguet, René. "L'Histoire Lausiaque, une oeuvre écrite dans l'esprit d'Évagre." *Revue d'Histoire Ecclésiastique*, 41 (1946): 321–364; 42 (1947): 5–49.

Driscoll, Jeremy. "Evagrius and Paphnutius on the causes for abandonment by God." *Studia Monastica*, 39.2 (1997): 259–86.

Elm, Suzanna. "Evagrius Ponticus' *Sententiae ad Virginem*." *Dumbarton Oaks Papers*, 45 (1991): 265–95.

Evagrius of Pontus. *De diversis malignis cogitationibus*. PG 79.

————. *Gnostikos*, ed. Antoine Guillaumont, *Évagre le Pontique: Le Gnostique ou a celui qui est devenu digne de la science*. SC 356; Paris: Cerf, 1989.

————. *De jejunio*, ed. and trans. J. Muyldermans, *Evagriana Syriaca: Textes inédits du British Museum et de la Vaticane*. Louvain: Publications Universitaires/Institut Orientaliste, 1952.

————. "Letter to Melania," trans. Martin Parmentier, "Evagrius of Pontus' 'Letter to Melania.' " *Bijdragen, tijdschrift voor filosofie en theologie*, 46 (1985): 2–38.

————. *Praktikos*, ed. A. and C. Guillaumont, *Évagre le Pontique: Traité pratique ou le moine*. SC 170–71; Paris: Cerf, 1971.

————. *The Praktikos [and] Chapters on Prayer*, trans. John Eudes Bamberger. Kalamazoo: Cistercian, 1981.

————. *Scholia on Ecclesiastes*, ed Paul Géhin, *Évagre le Pontique: Scholies à l'Ecclésiaste*. SC 397; Paris: Cerf, 1993.

————. *Scholia on Proverbs*, ed Paul Géhin, *Évagre le Pontique: Scholies aux Proverbes*. SC 340; Paris: Cerf, 1987.

Evelyn White, Hugh G., ed. Walter Hauser. *The Monasteries of the Wâdi 'n Natrûn*. 3 vols.; New York: Metropolitan Museum of Art, 1926–1933 (repr. Arno Press: New York, 1973). Part I: *New Coptic Texts from the Monastery of Saint Macarius*, Part II: *The History of the Monasteries of Nitria and Scetis*, Part III: *The Architecture and Archaeology*.

Festugière, A.-J. *Sainte Thècle, Saints Côme et Damien, Saints Cyr et Jean (extraits), Saint Georges*. Paris, 1971.

Florovsky, Georges. "Theophilus of Alexandria and Apa Aphou of Pemdje," in *Harry Austryn Wolfson Jubilee Volume* (Jerusalem: American Academy for Jewish Research, 1965), I: 275–310; repr. in Georges Florovsky, *Collected Works*, vol. 4, *Aspects of Church History* (Belmont, MA: Nordland, 1975): 97–129.

Frankfurter, David. *Religion in Roman Egypt: Assimilation and Resistance.* Princeton: Princeton University Press, 1998.

Gendle, Nicholas. "Cappadocian elements in the mystical theology of Evagrius Ponticus." *Studia Patristica*, 16, 373–84.

Goehring, James E. *Ascetics, Society, and the Desert: Studies in Early Egyptian Monasticism.* Studies in Antiquity and Christianity; Harrisburg, PA: Trinity, 1999.

Gould, Graham. *The Desert Fathers on Monastic Community.* Oxford: Clarendon, 1993.

————. "The Image of God and the Anthropomorphite Controversy in Fourth Century Monasticism," in Robert J. Daley, ed., *Origeniana Quinta*, 549–65. Leuven: University Press, 1992.

Grossmann, Peter. "The Pilgrimage Center of Abû Mînâ," in David Frankfurter, ed., *Pilgrimage and Holy Space in Late Antique Egypt*, 281–302. Leiden: Brill, 1998.

Guillaumont, Antoine. *Les "Kephalaia Gnostica" d'Évagre le Pontique et l'histoire de l'origénisme chez les Grecs et chez les Syriens.* Patristica Sorboniensia, 5; Paris, 1962.

————. *Aux origines du monachisme chrétien.* Spiritualité Orientale, 30; Solesmes: Bellefontaine, 1979

————. "L'Enseignement spirituel des moines d'Égypte," repr. in his *Études sur la spiritualité de l'orient chrétien*, 81–92. Bégrolles-en-Mauges: Bellefontaine, 1996.

————. "The Jesus Prayer Among the Monks of Egypt." *Eastern Churches Review*, 6 (1974): 66–71.

————. "Le problème des deux Macaires dans les *Apophthegmata Patrum*." *Irénikon*, 48 (1975): 41–59.

————. "Macarius the Egyptian, Saint," *The Coptic Encyclopedia*, ed. Aziz S. Atiya, 5.1491. New York: Doubleday, 1991.

Guy, Jean-Claude, ed. *Les Apophtegmes des Pères: Collection systématique. Chapitres I–IX.* SC 387; Paris: Cerf, 1993.

Hanson, R. P. C. *The Search for the Christian Doctrine of God.* Edinburgh: T & T Clark, 1988.

Harvey, Jr., Paul B., trans. "Jerome: Life of Paul, the First Hermit," in Vincent L. Wimbush, ed., *Ascetic Behavior in Greco-Roman Antiquity: A Sourcebook*, 357–69. Minneapolis: Fortress, 1990.

Heussi, Karl. *Der Ursprung des Mönchtums.* Tübingen, 1936.

Judge, E. A. "The Earliest Use of Monachos for 'Monk' (P. Coll. Youtie 77) and the Origins of Monasticism." *Jahrbuch für Antike und Christentum*, 20 (1977): 72–89.

Kelly, J. N. D. *Early Christian Creeds*. London: Longmans, 1950.

————. *Golden Mouth: The Story of John Chrysostom*. Ithaca: Cornell University Press, 1995.

Kraus, J. "Hierakas." *Lexikon für Theologie und Kirche*, 5.321. 2nd ed.; Freiburg, 1957.

Lampe, G. W. H. *A Patristic Greek Lexicon*. Oxford: Clarendon, 1961.

Layton, Bentley. "Social Structure and Food Consumption in an Early Christian Monastery: The Evidence of Shenoute's Canons and the White Monastery Federation A.D. 385–465." *Le Muséon*, 115.1–2 (2002): 25–57.

Lohse, Bernhard. *Askese und Mönchtum in der Anrike und in der alten Kirche*. Munich, 1969.

Meinardus, Otto F.A. *Monks and Monasteries of the Egyptian Deserts*. Rev. ed.; Cairo: AUC Press, 1992.

el-Meskeen, Matta. *Coptic Monasticism and the Monastery of St. Macarius: A Short History*. Cairo: the Monastery of St. Macarius, 1984.

Mikhail, Maged S., and Tim Vivian, trans. "Life of Saint John the Little." *Coptic Church Review*, 18.1–2 (1997): 3–64.

Molinier, Nicolas. *Ascèse, contemplation et ministère d'après l'Histoire Lausiaque de Pallade d'Hélénopolis*. Spiritualité orientale 64; Bégrolles-en-Mauges: Bellefontaine, 1995.

Moschus, John. *Pratum spirituale. The Spiritual Meadow of John Moschus*, trans. John Wortley. Kalamazoo: Cistercian, 1992.

Müller, Liguori G. *The De Haeresibus of Saint Augustine*. Washington, D.C.: The Catholic University of America Press, 1956.

Murphy, Francis X. *Rufinus of Aquileia (345–411): His Life and Works*. Washington, D.C.: Catholic University of America Press, 1945.

————. "Melania the Elder: A Biographical Note," *Traditio*, 5 (1947): 59–77.

————. "Evagrius Ponticus and Origenism," in Richard Hanson and Henri Crouzel, eds., *Origeniana Tertia*, 253–69. Rome: Edizioni dell' Ateneo, 1985.

Muyldermans, Joseph. "Evagriana Coptica." *Le Muséon*, 76 (1963): 271–76.

O'Laughlin, Michael. "Origenism in the Desert." Th.D. Thesis, Harvard University, 1987.

_____. "The Anthropology of Evagrius Ponticus and its Sources," in C. Kannengiesser and W. Petersen, eds., *Origen of Alexandria: His World and His Legacy*, 357–73. Notre Dame: Univ. of Notre Dame Press, 1988.

Orban, Myriam, ed. *Déserts chrétiens d'Égypte*. Nice: Culture Sud, 1993.

Palladius. *Dialogus de vita S. Joannis Chrysostomi*, ed. P. R. Coleman-Norton. Cambridge: Cambridge University Press, 1928.

_____. *Palladius: Dialogue on the Life of St. John Chrysostom*, trans. Robert T. Meyer. Ancient Christian Writers, 45; New York and Mahwah: Newman, 1985.

_____. *The Lausiac History of Palladius*, ed. and trans. Cuthbert Butler. 2 vols.; Cambridge: Cambridge University Press, 1898 and 1904.

_____. *The Lausiac History*, ed. G. J. M. Bartelink, *Palladio: La Storia Lausiaca*. Milan: Fondazione Lorenzo Valla, 1974.

_____. *The Lausiac History*, trans. Robert T. Meyer. Ancient Christian Writers 34; New York: Newman, 1965.

Papini, Lucia, and David Frankfurter. "Fragments of the *Sortes Sanctorum* from the Shrine of St. Colluthus," in Frankfurter, ed., *Pilgrimage and Holy Space in Late Antique Egypt*, 393–401. Leiden: Brill, 1998.

Rahlfs, Alfred, ed. *Septuaginta*. Stuttgart: Deutsche Bibelstiftung Stuttgart, 1935.

Regnault, Lucien. *Les Sentences des Pères du désert: Troisieme recueil et tables*. Solesmes, Bellefontaine, 1976.

_____. *Les Sentences des pères du désert: série des anonymes*. Solesmes: Bellefontaine, 1985.

_____. *La vie quotidienne des pères du désert en Égypte au IVe siècle*. Paris: Hachette, 1990. Eng. trans. *The Day-to-Day Life of the Desert Fathers in Fourth-Century Egypt*. Petersham, MA: Saint Bede's, 1999.

_____. "Quelques apophthegmes arabes sur la 'Prière de Jésus,'" *Irénikon*, 52 (1979): 344–55.

_____. "La prière continuelle 'monologistos' dans la littérature apophtegmatique." *Irénikon*, 47 (1974): 467–93. Reprinted in *Les Pères du désert à travers leur Apophtegmes*, 113–39. Solesmes, 1987.

Russell, Norman, trans. *The Lives of the Desert Fathers: The Historia Monachorum in Aegypto*. Kalamazoo: Cistercian, 1980.

Solari, Placid. "Christ as Virtue in Didymus the Blind," in Harriet A. Luckman and Linda Kulzer, eds., *Purity of Heart in Early Ascetic and Monastic Literature*, 67–88. Collegeville: Liturgical Press, 1999.

Stewart, Columba. "Radical Honesty about the Self: the Practice of the Desert Fathers." *Sobornost*, 12 (1990): 25–39.

———. "Feature Review: Three Recent Studies on Ancient Monasticism." *American Benedictine Review*, 50.1 (1999), 3–11.

———. "Imageless Prayer and the Theological Vision of Evagrius Ponticus." *Journal of Early Christian Studies*, 9:2 (2001): 173–204.

Strothmann, Werner, ed. *Die syrische Überlieferung der Schriften des Makarios*. 2 vols.; Wiesbaden: Harrossowitz, 1981.

Swanson, Mark N. " 'These Three Words Will Suffice': The 'Jesus Prayer' in Coptic Tradition," *Parole de l'Orient*, 25 (2000): 695–714.

Theodoret. *Religious History*, trans. R. M. Price, *A History of the Monks of Syria*. Kalamazoo: Cistercian, 1985.

Timbie, Janet. "A Liturgical Procession in the Desert of Apa Shenoute," in David Frankfurter, ed., *Pilgrimage and Holy Space in Late Antique Egypt*, 415–41. Leiden: Brill, 1998.

Toda, Satoshi. "La Vie de S. Macaire l'Égyptien: État de la question." *Analecta Bollandiana*, 118:3–4 (2000): 267–90.

Turner, C. H. "Palladiana II: The Lausiac History. Questions of History." *Journal of Theological Studies*, 22 (1921): 21–35, 138–55.

van Esbroeck, Michel. "La dormition chez les coptes," *Actes du IVe Congrès Copte, Louvain-la-Neuve, 5–10 Sept. 1988*, ed. M. Rassart-Debergh et J. Ries, 436–45. Publications de l'Institut Orientaliste de Louvain 41; Louvain-la-Neuve: Institut Orientaliste, 1992. Repr. in van Esbroeck, *Aux origines de la Dormition de la Vierge: Etudes historiques sur les traditions orientales*, XI.436–45. Collected Studies Series 472; Aldershot: Variorum, 1995.

Veilleux, Armand, ed., *Pachomian Koinonia*. Kalamazoo: Cistercian, 1980.

Vivian, Tim. *Paphnutius: Histories of the Monks of Upper Egypt and the life of Onnophrius*. Kalamazoo: Cistercian, 1993.

———. *Journeying into God*. Minneapolis: Fortress, 1996.

———. "Words to Live By: 'A Conversation that the Elders Had with One Another Concerning Thoughts (ΠΕΡΙ ΛΟΓΙΣΜΩΝ).'" *St. Vladimir's Theological Quarterly*, 39:2 (1995): 127–41.

———. "The Good God, the Holy Power, and the Paraclete: 'To the Sons of God' (*Ad filios Dei*) by Saint Macarius the Great." *Anglican Theological Review*, 30.3 (1998): 338–65.

————. "The Monasteries of the Wadi Natrun, Egypt: A Personal and Monastic Journey." *American Benedictine Review* 49:1 (March 1998): 3–32.

Vivian, Tim, and Apostolos N. Athanassakis, trans., *The Life of Saint George of Choziba*. San Francisco: ISP, 1994.

————. *The Life of Antony*. Kalamazoo: Cistercian, 2003.

Vivian, Tim, and Birger A. Pearson. "Saint Paul of Tamma on the Monastic Cell (de Cella)," *Hallel*, 23.2 (1998): 86–107.

Vogt, Kari. "The Coptic Practice of the Jesus Prayer: A Tradition Revived," 111–20 in Nelly Van Doorn-Harder and Kari Vogt, eds., *Between Desert and City: The Coptic Orthodox Church Today*. Oslo: Novus forlag, 1997.

Vogüé, Adalbert de. "Les fragments coptes de l'Histoire Lausiaque: l'édition d'Amélineau et le manuscrit." *Orientalia*, 58.3 (1989): 326–32.

————. "La version copte du chapitre XVII de l'Histoire Lausiaque: Les deux éditeurs et les trois manuscrits." *Orientalia*, 58.4 (1989): 510–24.

————. "Le texte copte du chapitre XVIII de l'Histoire Lausiaque: L'édition d'Amélineau et le manuscrit." *Orientalia*, 61.4 (1992): 459–62.

Ward, Benedicta, trans. *The Sayings of the Desert Fathers: The Alphabetical Collection*. Rev. ed.; Kalamazoo: Cistercian, 1984.

Ware, Kallistos. "The Origins of the Jesus Prayer: Diadochus, Gaza, Sinai," in Cheslyn Jones, Geoffrey Wainwright, Edward Yarnold, eds., *The Study of Spirituality*, 175–184. New York: Oxford University Press, 1986.

Williams, Rowan. *The Wound of Knowledge: Christian Spirituality from the New Testament to St. John of the Cross*. Cambridge, MA: Cowley, 1991.